Citizen Rights, Migrant Rights and Civic Stratification

I0041581

This book explores the concept of civic stratification and examines its contemporary relevance for analysis and understanding of the functioning of rights in society.

David Lockwood's (1996) concept of civic stratification outlines the way in which the rights associated with citizenship can be a source of inequality by virtue of their formal granting or denial by the state, or by informal impediments to their full realisation. The purpose of this book is to explore the meaning and significance of this concept, and elaborate its potential in offering a framework for understanding the dynamic nature of rights. Lockwood's model reverses Marshall's (1950) view of citizenship as guaranteed inclusion in society and is linked to the way that the differential entitlement and the qualifying conditions associated with certain rights can be harnessed as a means of control. While both Marshall and Lockwood were principally concerned with the rights attaching to citizenship, this book extends the insights of these two authors to show how such controls apply in various ways to both citizens and non-citizens alike. Building on Lockwood's conception of 'moral resources' the book set out a theoretical framework and empirical illustration of how the position of different groups within society is subject to shifting perceptions of social worth and is engaged both in claims to fuller access to rights and in justifications of their denial or removal.

This book will appeal to scholars and higher-level students with relevant interests in sociolegal studies, sociology, social policy and politics.

Lydia Morris is Professor of Sociology at the University of Essex, UK.

Citizen Rights, Migrant Rights and Civic Stratification

Lydia Morris

Routledge
Taylor & Francis Group
a GlassHouse Book

First published 2025
by Routledge
4 Park Square, Milton Park, Abingdon, Oxon OX14 4RN

and by Routledge
605 Third Avenue, New York, NY 10158

Routledge is an imprint of the Taylor & Francis Group, an informa business

A GlassHouse book

This publication was supported by the University of Essex's open access fund.

British Library Cataloguing-in-Publication Data
A catalogue record for this book is available from the British Library

ISBN: 9781032349817 (hbk)
ISBN: 9781032349831 (pbk)
ISBN: 9781003324744 (ebk)

DOI: 10.4324/9781003324744

Typeset in Times New Roman
by Deanta Global Publishing Services, Chennai, India

In memory of David Lockwood.

Contents

Abbreviations

A1P1	Article 1 Protocol 1 (of the ECHR)
APPG	All Party Parliamentary Group
CAP	Church Action on Poverty
CESCR	Committee on Economic Social and Cultural Rights
CPAG	Child Poverty Action Group
CRC	Convention on the Rights of the Child
CSR	Convention on the Status of Refugees
DWP	Department of Work and Pensions
ECHR	Economic Convention on Human Rights
ECtHR	European Court of Human Rights
EEA	European Economic Area
EU	European Union
EWCA	England and Wales Court of Appeal
EWHC	England and Wales High Court
HRA	Human Rights Act
ICESCR	International Covenant on Economic Social and Cultural Rights
JCWI	Joint Council for the Welfare of Immigrants
LBC	London Broadcasting Company
MAC	Migration Advisory Committee
NABA	Nationality and Borders Act
NGO	Non-governmental Organisation
NHS	National Health Service
NRPF	No Recourse to Public Funds
OHCHR	Office of the High Commissioner for Human Rights
ONS	Office of National Statistics
PCC	Press Complaints Commission
PNG	Papua New Guinea
RAF	Royal Air Force
SIAC	Special Immigration Appeals Commission
SSHD	Secretary of State for the Home Department
SSWP	Secretary of State for Work and Pensions
TUC	Trades Union Congress

UDHR	Universal Declaration of Human Rights
UKHL	United Kingdom House of Lords
UKSC	United Kingdom Supreme Court
UKUT	United Kingdom Upper Tribunal
UNCLOS	United Nations Convention on the Law of the Sea
UNHCR	United Nations High Commission for Refugees
WCA	Work Capability Assessment
WRAG	Work Related Activity Group

Introduction

This book is about the differential granting of rights, which in its most basic form distinguishes between citizens and non-citizens, the latter group being principally made up of trans-national migrants. As we will see, this distinction is just the beginning of a complex system for the unequal distribution of rights, which can be usefully analysed through the concept of civic stratification. In outlining this concept, David Lockwood (1996) sets out the way that the rights associated with citizenship can be a source of inequality by virtue of their formal granting or denial by the state, or by informal impediments to their full realisation. The purpose of the present book is to explore the meaning and significance of this concept, and elaborate its potential in offering a framework for understanding the dynamic nature of rights in relation to both citizens and migrants.

Lockwood's model reverses Marshall's [1950] (1973) view of citizenship as guaranteed inclusion in society to ask how and how far citizenship is implicated in the construction of social inequality. As we will see, this question can also be linked to the way the differential entitlement and the qualifying conditions associated with certain rights can be harnessed as a means of control. While both Marshall and Lockwood were principally concerned with the rights attaching to citizenship, this book will extend the insights of these two authors to show how such controls apply in various ways to both citizens and non-citizens alike. Notions of the worthy and unworthy pervade both historical and contemporary analyses of access to rights, particularly social (welfare) rights. However, by building on Lockwood's conception of 'moral resources' this book will set out a theoretical framework and empirical illustration of how the position of different groups within society is subject to shifting perceptions of social worth, which are also engaged both in claims to fuller access to rights, and in justifications of their denial or removal.

There has been growing interest in the sociological significance of rights over a period of roughly 30 years. This has been linked in part to a disenchantment with class politics, the challenges of securing social inclusion, the growing social and political significance of trans-national migration, optimism about cosmopolitan forces and the promise of 'universals', and conversely a

DOI: 10.4324/9781003324744-1

degree of scepticism about their actual realisation. There have been significant analytical advances with respect to each of these topics, but no consolidated attempt to bring them together within a single field of study – the sociology of rights. T.H. Marshall's [1950] (1973) *Citizenship and Social Class* was perhaps the first attempt to build a sociology of rights, based on the idea of citizenship as a guarantee of membership in the community (p.92), or we might say social inclusion. However, Lockwood's (1996:536) more recent argument that 'the ethos and practice of citizenship is at least as likely as class relations to structure group interests and thereby fields of conflict and discontent' offers further untapped potential, most notably through an elaboration of the concept of civic stratification.

Civic stratification can be defined as a system of inequality by virtue of the granting, denial or unequal realisation of rights, as shaped by state interventions and mediated by political discourse, public sentiment and social movements. While references to the deserving and undeserving, shirkers and strivers and the stratified nature of non-citizens rights have become commonplace, they are rarely accompanied by a full elaboration of the conceptual framework implied. The idea of civic stratification has been applied in my own writing to the analysis of migrant rights, and has been adopted by a number of other writers, but without a comprehensive treatment of the huge potential that the concept holds. The elaboration of this potential is a key feature of the present book, which will look at the original set of interests that informed the notion, and at how subsequent developments have made it ever more relevant to the analysis of our times. As we will see, such analysis engages not only citizenship guarantees, but also welfare rights and requirements, the management of migration, the claims of asylum seekers and the significance of boundary drawing in each of these fields.

The book begins with a conceptual chapter that sets out the background to civic stratification with reference to Marshall's model of citizenship, and the analytical advances made by Lockwood, while also noting Marx's [1843] (1975) observations on the limits of citizenship guarantees. Subsequent chapters each focus on a key substantive aspect of rights, respectively addressing domestic welfare, international migration and asylum, both in terms of the conceptual elaboration of Lockwood's model and in terms of its use in analysing the practice of rights. A final chapter will outline the way civic stratification can connect to and illuminate contemporary debate in related fields – notably cosmopolitanism, governance, recognition, moral economy, bordering, topology and the erosion of citizenship.

Chapter 1 – The conceptual grounding of civic stratification: T.H. Marshall's [1950] (1973) famous essay on 'Citizenship and Social Class' offered what might be termed the first sociological approach to citizenship, which he views as a formally equal status and an expression of social worth that could secure 'a kind of basic human equality, associated with full community membership' (p.45). However, Lockwood's (1996) concept of 'civic stratification' reverses Marshall's argument by pointing to the inequalities that can arise from the operation of citizenship, and he considers the ways in which citizenship is both embedded in, and also contributes to, the structure of social inequality. Hence, his argument seeing citizenship as a likely focus for group actions that test and contest the boundaries of rights, in a manner akin to class mobilisation.

This possibility was in some sense already recognised by Marx [1843] (1975) in his discussion of 'the Jewish question', but Lockwood's more explicit formulation lies at the heart of the extensive agenda engaged by the concept of civic stratification. The term encapsulates an approach to rights as both enabling and controlling devices, and hence open to both expansive and restrictive dynamics, as shaped by state policy and discourse, and mediated by the interventions of civic activists. Lockwood's elaboration rests on the construction of a matrix that sets out the dynamic nature of the relationship between the formal possession of rights, and the informal influence of moral and material resources. The first chapter outlines this basic framework, while later chapters show how it yields a model whose implications go far beyond Lockwood's initial orienting argument.

Chapter 2 – Welfare as social inclusion or stratified control?: This chapter focuses on the core element of Marshall's guarantee of social inclusion, which rests quite heavily on social rights as 'a right to share to the full in the social heritage and to live the life of a civilised being according to the standards prevailing in the society.' (p.8) Social rights for Marshall thus imply 'an absolute right…conditional only on the discharge of the general duties of citizenship.' (p.26), but for Lockwood the more firmly absolute nature of civil and political rights has meant that 'the endemic contradiction between citizenship and capital has so far been managed by the fine tuning of social rights' (p.535). However, at the heart of his own analysis lies the question of 'under which conditions inequality is tolerated or rejected' (p.531), thus turning Marshall's guarantee into a more malleable proposition.

The substantive application of these ideas is fleshed out in this chapter by an examination of key moments in the British welfare system – itself the basis for Marshall's model of citizenship. Here we find that the fine-tuning referred to by Lockwood is achieved by the increasing elaboration of conditional requirements attached to the receipt of social rights, and justified by an associated moral discourse, thus constituting a distinctive 'moral economy'. The effect is to stratify the experience of claimants both in terms of their formal entitlement, by virtue of the degree of conditionality attached, while correspondingly heightening the degree of stigma and negative moral standing associated with particular types of claim. The chapter moves on from this argument to consider the implications of universal human rights obligations, both for the delivery of citizens' social rights and for Lockwood's civic stratification model.

Chapter 3 – Civic stratification and migration: This chapter begins with a common criticism of Marshall's approach (see Anthias and Yuval-Davis, 1992) – his neglect to consider the boundaries of citizenship. Although his definition turns on the idea of 'full community membership' (p.45) he does not address the question of how the boundaries of the community or of membership are drawn. Though Lockwood (1996) is principally concerned with the inequalities generated by the internal functioning of citizenship, he does gesture to its external effects in denying full inclusion for those who lack the formal status, even when lawfully present on national territory. He makes this point in reference to the ethnic stigma and partial civic exclusion experienced by *'gastarbeiter'* (guestworkers), but offers little further elaboration.

However, the substantive application of this insight then shows how the concept of civic stratification admirably lends itself to analysis of the growing incidence of what Brubaker (1989) has termed positions of 'partial membership' and the *ad hoc* proliferation of lesser statuses. Hence, stratified rights emerge as the means of mediating an apparent contradiction between the continuing significance of national citizenship and the growing purchase of transnational rights – sometimes construed as an emergent post-national society (Soysal, 1994). We see how steps to limit rights are commonly driven by an assault on 'moral standing' but may also be met by recourse to universalist claims, though even universal human rights may have qualifying conditions attached. The outcome can aptly be viewed through the lens of civic stratification, with particular attention to the interactions between its formal and informal components.

Chapter 4 – Civic stratification and asylum: There are various ways in which the concept of civic stratification can be applied to the treatment of asylum seekers, a category whose very presence on national territory depends on the engagement of international guarantees, most notably the commitment to *non-refoulement* contained in the Refugee Convention (United Nations High Commission for Refugees (UNHCR), 1951). Although this obligation is itself absolute, the claim for asylum can be met by differing degrees of protection, not only full refugee status but humanitarian leave, a right to remain on human rights grounds, or discretionary presence, and of course rejection of the claim. However, even full recognition as a refugee is less than completely secure, and states increasingly activate safe return reviews after the initial grant of residence. There are also various aspects of the associated rights that are to some degree open to negotiation and manipulation, and these will be illustrated in Chapter 4 by substantive examples.

So the chapter looks to instances of policy designed to create different categories of asylum seekers, which might be determined by country of origin or degrees of 'vulnerability' (as with Britain's Syrian resettlement scheme), or by mode of arrival – as with the 2002 denial of welfare for in-country claimants, or plans in Britain (current at the time of writing) to process 'unlawful' arrivals outside national territory. Other forms of stratified rights apply to shifting levels of maintenance – currently set at around half of mainstream welfare rates in Britain, while recognised refugees with full welfare rights often suffer a deficit when it comes to making a claim from the mainstream system. All such patterns of entitlement show complex interactions with political discourse and public sentiments, both reflecting and shaping the moral standing of the claimants concerned.

Chapter 5 – Civic stratification and sociological debate: This final chapter reviews the analytical potential of the concept of civic stratification, and the advances that can be made by linking the concept more explicitly to a range of other debates. So here we broaden the framework by making a fuller connection with allied debates that have not thus far engaged with the concept of civic stratification. We therefore consider the cosmopolitan promise and post-national predictions of an opening up of rights beyond citizenship, while weighing them against the constraints imposed by civic stratification. This leads on to a consideration of rights as a form of governance and means of control, which can also be considered alongside rights as a form of recognition. In both cases, political discourse will often harness a particular moral vision, or 'moral economy', that provides the justificatory framework for any given regime of rights. Restrictive regimes will nevertheless be open to contestation and change, often driven by 'cosmopolitan' or 'post-national' sentiments, while the disciplinary and controlling dimension of rights is closely associated with what has been termed the practice of 'bordering'.

In each case, related arguments could be enriched by elaborating their implicit connection with civic stratification: in mapping and analysis of the ever-shifting topology of rights, in exploring the discursive justifications for denial or contraction of rights, and in documenting the intervention of 'civic activists', who can bring their own moral resources to bear in a push for expansion. So to summarise what an analysis of civic stratification can bring to such a debate, first comes the recognition that formal legal entitlements can be stratified by the terms and conditions attached to claiming a right, and that this applies both with respect to different categories of migrant and also domestic welfare claimants. Secondly, we find a link between rights and moral standing – such that a granting of rights confirms moral worth, while a denial of rights can place moral worth in question. Thirdly, there is a likely connection between these two dimensions of civic stratification, which can fuel both expansion and contraction in a regime of rights. The book overall will therefore offer an elaboration and extension of Lockwood's (1996:547) claim that:

> while its practice is heavily influenced by the structure of class and status inequality, citizenship can be seen to exert a force-field of its own: in part through stratifying practices such as civic exclusion and stigmatization; in part through ethical exploitation as in civic activism.

References

Anthias, F. and N. Yuval-Davis (1992) *Racialised Boundaries*, Abingdon: Routledge

Brubaker, W.R. (1989) *Immigration and the Politics of Citizenship in Europe and America*, Lanham, MD: University Press of America

Lockwood, D. (1996) 'Civic integration and class formation' *British Journal of Sociology* 47(3):531–50

Marshall, T.H. [1950] (1973) *Citizenship and Social Class*, in *Class, Citizenship and Social Development*, New York: Doubleday and Co., pp.65–122

Marx, K. [1943] (1975) 'On the Jewish question' in *Karl Marx and Frederick Engels: Collected Works*, Volume 3, New York: International Publishers, pp.146–74

Soysal, Y. (1994) *The Limits of Citizenship*, Chicago: University of Chicago Press

UNHCR (1951) *Convention Relating to the Status of Refugees*, 496365eb2.pdf (unhcr .org) (accessed 23.2.24)

1 The conceptual grounding of civic stratification

A grasp of the conceptual grounding of civic stratification inevitably starts from T.H. Marshall's [1950] (1973) famous essay on 'Citizenship and Social Class', which may be seen as a first attempt to construct a sociology of rights. This opening chapter sets out a number of puzzling features that emerge from a close reading of Marshall's essay and the analytical and empirical agenda that they imply. After reviewing the basic contours of Marshall's argument, we move onto the unresolved issues embedded in his work, and the ways in which they are taken up and advanced in Lockwood's elaboration of civic stratification.

Marshall makes explicit a hypothesis that is latent in the work of Alfred Marshall, to the effect that: 'the inequality of the social class system may be acceptable provided the equality of citizenship is recognised' (Marshall, [1950] 1973:70). This possibility is then explored in his essay, which sees a modern drive for equality as the latest phase in an evolution of citizenship that has been in 'continuous progress for some 250 years' (p.71). However, along with the reference to *continuous* progress, the essay also raises the question of whether there are limits to the amelioration of class differences beyond which we cannot pass. The evolutionary phases Marshall speaks of are extracted from a historical account of how the basic rights associated with British citizenship unfolded through the granting of civil rights, political rights and social rights. These rights were respectively secured in the 18th, 19th and 20th centuries, and supported by the associated institutions of the courts, parliament and local authorities, and educational and social (welfare) provisions.

Citizenship is then conceived as both a formally equal status and an (informal) expression of social worth that could secure 'a kind of basic human equality, associated with full community membership' (p.117). The claim to this status is seen as 'a claim to be admitted to a share in the social heritage... a claim to be accepted as full members of the society' (p.69–70). There are some subtle shifts in Marshall's argument, however, and while he states: 'we are...proceeding at present on the assumption that the hypothesis (put forward by Alfred Marshall) is valid' (Marshall, [1950] 1973:117), the claim is modified by his view that 'the preservation of economic inequalities has been

DOI: 10.4324/9781003324744-2

made more difficult by the enrichment of the status of citizenship'. He also notes that: 'status differences can receive the stamp of legitimacy...provided that they do not cut too deep but occur within a population united in a single civilization' (p.116).

In fact, there are a number of unresolved issues (both implicit and explicit) in his essay that invite further attention, the central one being the relationship between the ostensible equality signalled by citizenship status and the persistence of class inequality. While Marshall acknowledges the role of civil rights in establishing the freedoms required by a competitive market economy, he nevertheless presents citizenship as the invasion of contract by status and as posing a possible conflict of principles. He revises his earlier comment that 20th century citizenship was at war with the class system [1950] (1973:110), taking instead the view that the former has imposed modifications on the latter, with social rights subordinating market price to social justice. However, the basic conflict between social rights and market value remained in his view unresolved (p.114), and he adds that citizenship itself becomes the architect of social inequality. This occurs by virtue of opportunities for all through education and training, such that 'citizenship operates as an instrument of social stratification' (p.110) but bears the stamp of legitimacy, and indeed 'the single uniform status of citizenship provided the foundation of equality on which the structure of inequality could be built' (p.88).

So Marshall seems to conclude that a compromise has been struck between potentially 'warring' principles, leaving open the question of how that compromise is reached, what form it takes and who is party to the negotiation. This leads on to a further question as to how citizenship rights have unfolded – by an inherent evolutionary dynamic, or by social struggle? One common criticism of Marshall (e.g. Mann, 1987; Turner, 1986) has been directed at the evolutionary assumptions contained within his model. However, a close reading of his text reveals recurrent references to the *struggles* involved in the quest for rights – a fight against parliament for individual liberty, an attack on monopolies by the Common Law, a battle between 'the old and the new' in the assertion of social rights, etc. Such comments then raise a series of questions about the dynamic unfolding of rights, how struggles are brought about, and how expansion may be 'stimulated both by the struggle to win rights, and by their enjoyment once won' (Marshall, [1950] 1973:92). So we are left with a question as to the limit of the 'urge forward' towards a full measure of equality that Marshall identifies, and of whether forward progress is inevitable, or could in fact be reversed.

Another set of questions arises in relation to Marshall's use of the concept of status, and its central role in his argument about the guarantee of full membership in society. It is helpful here to make reference to Marshall's note on status (1973a) and his elaboration of the definition provided by C.K. Allen. Allen sees status as 'the condition of belonging to a particular class of persons to whom the law assigns peculiar legal capacities or incapacities or both' (cited in Marshall, 1973a:205). Marshall adds to this his view that sociologists are correct to extend the meaning of this concept from a narrow legal conception to 'socially recognised rights and duties and so to socially accepted behaviour' (p.205). This is then the source of his belief that citizenship acts as both a legal status and a conferment of individual social worth – sometimes construed as a form of 'recognition' (see Honneth, 1995) – which is grounded in the 'basic human equality' that Marshall refers to. So while social rights provoke a conflict between market value and social justice, we might also see a related conflict to turn on the source of social recognition. In a society in which economic differences are the primary source of status, how then do we separate status from class position to ensure that 'basic human equality' takes precedence?

Class and status are also mutually implicated in another aspect of Marshall's [1950] (1973) argument that invites elaboration and reflection; the notion of legitimate inequality, and the associated argument that equal citizenship status provided 'the foundation of equality on which the structure of inequality could be built' (p.88). In discussing the Trades Union Congress' (TUC) recognition of a need to maintain such wage differentials as were required to sustain standards of 'craftsmanship' Marshall comments: 'here market value and economic incentive find a place in an argument which is fundamentally concerned with status' (p.114). He arrives at this view through an acceptance that the wage differentials of his time were rooted in tradition and custom, which are social not economic principles and were old names for the modern structure of status rights. Furthermore, he had previously asserted that 'what matters to the citizen is the superstructure of legitimate expectations' (p.104). There is a reference here to the 'qualitative element' of citizenship, and also a hint that citizenship guarantees must carry with them both state agreement and public sentiment in (re)shaping custom and tradition. In this process, 'the target is perpetually moving forward…[but] individual rights must be subordinated to national plans' (p.104). So while 'legitimate inequality' may be built upon equal citizenship status, the aim of equal citizenship may also need to be cultivated, and Barbalet (1988:82) notes that elsewhere in Marshall's work he sees a role for political propaganda in building loyalty to the state. We might suppose that this process would also feed into conceptions of 'legitimate' and 'illegitimate' claims to rights and recognition.

In fact, there is a suggestion in Marshall's essay that the 'urge forward' will not necessarily succeed and he makes a seemingly passing reference to 'the stratified status system which is creeping into citizenship' (p.111). His meaning here is not elaborated but there is also a later reference to 'some of the conflicts within our social system (that) are becoming too sharp for the compromise to achieve its purpose' (p.122). The nature of this conflict is clearly that between equality of status and inequality of class, but what of the stratified status that is creeping into citizenship, and note his observation cited earlier, that 'status differences can receive the stamp of legitimacy…provided they do not cut too deep, but occur within a population united in a single civilization' (p.116). So is he referring here to a class effect or something generated by the operations of citizenship itself?

There is some indication in Marshall's essay of the way that notionally equal rights may not be equally enjoyed, and though these comments are addressing the situation prior to an established system of social rights they do have continuing relevance. Marshall comments that civil rights confer a right to strive for possessions, and that a property right is not a right to possess property but a right to acquire it. He also notes that freedom of speech has little substance for those who lack the education necessary to fully realise such a right, and that equality before the law does not protect those for whom low income means that a remedy is out of reach (p.88). He has also recognised that class prejudice in the past coloured the whole administration of justice and that class intimidation interfered with the right to vote. These reservations about the failure of rights to fully deliver are not elaborated in his discussion of citizenship guarantees in his own era, given his optimistic view that 'class monopoly in politics has been overthrown', and his hopes for meaningful access to justice through legal aid. However, he does question whether the more contemporary promise of equal opportunity through education would be achieved in practice (p.107) and his essay indirectly draws attention to broader questions about practical impediments to the full enjoyment of rights.

So while Marshall sets out a general model of the potential role for citizenship in building a society united by loyalty to a common civilisation, there are a number of interesting issues embedded in his classic essay that would repay further attention. These include the nature of the relationship between citizenship and social class; the limits of compromise in the conflict of principles involved; whether the unfolding of rights is through an inherent (evolutionary) dynamic or is driven by struggle; whether the forward urge towards a full(er) citizenship has a limit; the significance of Marshall's two elements of status; the meaning of 'legitimate' inequality; the role of custom and public sentiment in building legitimacy (or its converse); the possible subordination of rights claims to state policy; the meaning of citizenship as the architect of inequality; the nature of the status system that is 'creeping into citizenship'; the source of the conflicts that are becoming 'too sharp'; the constraints on citizenship derived from national policy priorities; the practical impediments to the full enjoyment of rights; the nature and source of movement in a regime of rights; whether such movement is necessarily progressive; and finally, the position of the non-citizen – a matter that is not addressed in Marshall's essay.

All of these issues make an appearance in David Lockwood's (1996) elaboration of the concept of civic stratification, which in many respects picks up where Marshall left off. However, Lockwood reverses Marshall's problematic by focussing on the inequalities that can arise from the operation of citizenship, and he considers the ways in which citizenship is both embedded in and contributes to the structure of social inequality. This possibility was in some sense already recognised by Marx [1843] (1975:153), who argued that in proclaiming each member as an equal participant 'the state abolishes, in its own way, distinctions based on birth, social rank, education and occupation'. However, in allowing such distinctions to exist in civil society, it failed to guarantee the equal enjoyment of citizenship. With particular reference to 'the Jewish Question', whereby Jews in Germany in 1843 sought recognition from the German state, Marx's point was that 'political emancipation' alone was insufficient to secure equality, which rather required full 'human emancipation' (p.152). For him, even the 'so called rights of man' secured those civil freedoms that were necessary for the functioning of market capitalism; they recognised and defended the rights of 'egoistic man, of man separated from other men and from the community' (p.162) and their practical application was in defending a right to private property. So the telling question was whether social inequalities could be rendered irrelevant to the enjoyment of citizenship or should rather be abolished through social revolution, but for Marx any equalising effect of rights would be limited by the broader context of class inequality.

In fact, changes in western capitalist society in the 20th century raised the question of how far the working class had been incorporated into the structure of capitalism, thus undermining their revolutionary potential. In considering this debate Barbalet (1988:3) highlights two possibilities – that class conflict is displaced by other forms of antagonism, or class structures are so resistant to change that they persist and even infiltrate the functioning of citizenship. Marshall echoed something of Marx's sentiment in recognising that civil rights had been a necessary basis for the invasion of status by contract – and hence the break from feudalism – facilitating the construction of competitive market capitalism. The ensuing class inequalities are argued by Marshall to be offset by the recognition of equal worth conveyed by a uniform status of citizenship. However, Lockwood's more explicit and wider-ranging formulation of the inequalities contained within citizenship lies at the heart of the vast potential engaged by the concept of civic stratification.

Like Marshall, Lockwood is interested in the relationship between citizenship and social class, and he starts from the question of how far the integrative function of citizenship has succeeded. His appreciation of Marshall (Lockwood, 1974) traces the genesis of this question to Weber's theory of social stratification, which outlines 'the determination of life chances by the two opposing forces of market situation and status situation' (p.365). Lockwood also observes that Marshall brought the legal character of status group stratification back to 'due prominence' such that the idea of status differentiation refers not only to prestige ranking but also to the legally sanctioned structure of rights. Though this insight is drawn from Weber's argument, Lockwood notes that Weber gave no consideration to the 'new bases of citizenship status', which of course were Marshall's primary concern. He also observes that the integrative element of Marshall's argument has been overdrawn, and that the conflicting group interests that shape the institutional form of citizenship themselves have the potential for exacerbating as well as diminishing class conflict.

Lockwood's 1996 essay on civic stratification (titled 'Civic integration and class formation') starts from the observation that there are doubts about the continuing relevance of class war in the sense derived from Marx, and he therefore ponders what should take its place. He suggests reversing the question of how the class structure affects social integration, to ask 'how the institutional structure central to social integration affects class formation, and is perhaps even conducive to class de-formation' (p.532). This then is his lead-in to the concept of civic stratification, construed as 'the ways in which the structuring of life chances and social identities is the direct or indirect result of the institutionalisation of citizenship under conditions of social and economic inequality' (p.532). So like Marshall, Lockwood is interested in the integrative power of citizenship but addresses directly an issue only hinted at by Marshall – that citizenship itself could be a source of inequality. So his orienting claim is that: 'the impact on social integration of changes in class structure is not direct, but mediated by institutions that regulate and legitimate a much wider range of inequalities' (Lockwood, 1996:532). While Marshall's central conclusion is that the clash of principles between citizenship and social class is settled by compromise, the nature and effects of that compromise – or mediation in Lockwood's terms – now becomes the starting point for investigation. And note the idea of 'legitimate' inequality appears again, as in Marshall's essay.

Lockwood's guiding objective is therefore: 'to consider the consequences for social integration of the manner in which the institutionalisation of citizenship is embedded in, and at the same time contributes to, the structure of social inequality' (p.533). He also notes that the centrality of social stratification for the discipline of sociology lies in the question of 'under what conditions inequality is tolerated or rejected' (p.531), a question that speaks to the 'legitimacy' of inequality and therefore the limits of the compromise struck between class and citizenship. Hence, Lockwood reverses the thrust of Marshall's focus on the integrative power of citizenship, in a way that carries forward some of the questions identified above. Lockwood's interests concern the mediating role played by citizenship in relation to class inequality, the extent to which it both reflects existing inequality while also contributing to it, the degree of acceptability of inequality, and therefore its legitimacy. The source of the latter is argued to rest on the unity of market, bureaucratic and citizenship relations in that all individuals are subject to the same impersonal rules that legitimate the allocation to occupational positions and the differential rewards attached. The same is argued to apply to political rights, educational opportunities and the distribution of welfare benefits. So 'legitimate' inequality is taken to refer to those aspects of differential desert that are governed by impersonal rules of universal application – what Lockwood terms the 'universalistic rules of the game' (p.535).

Lockwood recognises the inevitable tension involved in negotiating the requirements of capital accumulation and the need to secure popular consent through welfare guarantees, sometimes provoking a 'fiscal crisis of the state' – and as we have seen Marshall also notes the constraint of national plans in overriding citizenship demands. One necessary element for managing this tension is an established agreement about the 'hierarchy of rewards', such that popular consent is part of the claim to 'legitimacy', and is governed by some 'rough notions of desert and merit' (1996:535). These issues speak to the nature and limits of the compromise between class inequality and the guarantees entailed in citizenship, while also giving a clearer indication of what is meant by legitimate inequality, and the significance of a broad popular consensus on 'the rules of the game'. However, since Lockwood assumes that civil and political rights are an absolute and basic requirement of capitalist liberal democracy, he notes that: 'the endemic contradiction between citizenship and capital has so far been managed by the fine-tuning of social rights' (p.535). The necessary compromise is then driven by some form of 'selectivity', most notably placing a value on 'individual achievement and self-responsibility', the other side of which is a condemnation of those who are assumed to have 'brought their ills upon themselves'. So here we have one means by which 'legitimate inequality' is constructed.

The point at which Lockwood most clearly moves beyond Marshall is in his proposition that: 'the ethos and practice of citizenship is at least as likely as class relations to structure group interests and thereby fields of conflict and discontent' (p.536). He relates this probability to the 'urge forward' identified by Marshall, adding that citizenship is an 'ideal whose actualisation is always less than complete' (p.536), and perhaps the most important aspect of his argument lies in the nature of this incompleteness. Hence, Lockwood argues that the citizenship ideal sets standards that have not yet been reached, while its delivery is commonly flawed by force of circumstance and vested interests. The crucial heart of his article is then built around this insight, and he offers a model for tracing four forms of civic stratification that emerge from the combination of Marshall's two dimensions of status. These are what Lockwood terms the possession or absence of rights, and the possession of moral and material resources – the former relates to a situation in which rights are (or are not) formally granted, and the latter to whether they are fully enjoyed. The meaning of material resources is self-evident and suggests a class dimension to the enjoyment of rights, while 'moral resources' are defined as 'advantages conferred by social standing and social networks, command of information, and general know-how, including the ability to attain one's ends through the activation of shared moral sentiments' (p.536). They therefore concern both the rules of the game governing merit and desert, and the variable ability of individuals to play that game. These two dimensions of status might also be construed as the formal (legal) dimension and the informal (social) dimension of citizenship.

This formulation builds on Marshall's insights but is an advance on the notion of citizenship as the architect of legitimate inequality, not least because it draws attention to the legitimating sentiments that govern status difference. So we might see legitimacy in terms of popular acceptance in relation to citizenship guarantees, and also those values relating to judgements about what we might term the moral standing of the individual citizen. A weak moral standing would then relate to the absence of moral resources, to markers of 'demerit', or to an erosion of moral standing deriving from the classic construal of particular categories as undeserving. However, Lockwood's elaboration of the four forms of civic stratification seems to go beyond the assumed legitimacy of these sentiments and moves into the terrain of *illegitimate* inequalities – through administrative failure in the impersonal application of the rules, or overt bias in the granting or delivery of rights.

Working from a 2 x 2 matrix, Lockwood (1996:536) is then in a position to document his *four forms* of civic stratification. These four possibilities show different combinations of what I have termed the formal and informal aspects of citizenship – the formal presence or absence of rights, and the informal possession of moral and material resources. Within the formal dimension, the absence of rights could, as Lockwood notes, refer to new rights that are aspired to but that have not yet been achieved or a lack by some groups of eligibility for already existing rights.

Civic exclusion – This occurs when a particular category is denied full citizenship rights or when existing rights are in some way overridden or abrogated; hence it refers to a formal exclusion. The best contemporary example would be international migrants who lack citizenship of their destination country, and especially those whose presence is 'undocumented'. Their position is only briefly touched on by Lockwood in his reference to *gastarbeiter* and the picture is more complex than this passing reference suggests, as discussed in Chapter 3 of this book. Other clear examples of exclusion are largely historical, and as Lockwood argues, are most 'glaringly offensive' (p.537) when members of the excluded group share some ascriptive feature such as gender, race or sexuality. So examples would be the denial of full civil and political rights for women at various points in the past (see Walby, 1997); the past denial of a public existence for homosexuals – extending *inter alia* to exclusion from public office, or the denial of the right to marry and found a family (Richardson, 1998); or the denial of basic civil and political rights for certain minorities, either by law or by failure to fully implement the law, as in the case of black voter registration in the US. These examples would feature in the chart above as an absence of rights, or what Lockwood terms 'civic disqualification of a fairly blatant kind: namely *de jure* or *de facto* exclusion' (p.537). They also go alongside an absence of moral or material resources, which means that such groups experience denigration in terms of public perceptions of their worth. This leads to what we can term a weak 'moral standing' in society and hence a lack of the moral resources that might enable contestation. Where rights are formally present but imperfectly delivered or enjoyed then exclusions shade over into the next category of civic deficit.

Civic deficit – Given the (albeit imperfect) advances of anti-discrimination legislation, contemporary examples of full civic exclusion are rare (though the position of undocumented migrants comes close). What might commonly be viewed as a denial of rights is more likely to take the form of a deficit by virtue of impediments to the full enjoyment or delivery of a right that is formally held. According to Lockwood, this refers to 'a situation in which a lack of resources prevents the exercise of rights that are formally enjoyed, or to one in which the exercise of rights is derogating' (p.537). We might add a third factor, when the administration or delivery of rights is negatively affected by covert prejudice, but for civic deficit as a whole the formal presence of rights is made less effective by a lack of moral or material resources that might compel more adequate delivery.

Lockwood subdivides deficit into three categories – power deficit, stigmatised deficit and fiscal deficit. His example of power deficit is the unequal balance of power between worker and employer in the notionally free and equal contract of employment. Another example would be problems of access to justice by virtue of the costs of legal action. Stigmatised deficit arises when the actual claim to a right itself places the claimant in a negative light – the example given by Lockwood is the operation of social citizenship (notably welfare rights), which itself creates a category of 'lesser citizens'. Their situation is at inception the product of a lack of material resources, but the very act of claiming support erodes their moral resources or moral standing in society, though this dynamic varies with the type of benefit claimed (see Laenen et al., 2019). The claimants' position of dependency means that their situation is status determined, though in the case of the unemployed it is also often a product of their class location. However, the outcome is a lack of 'moral leverage', while budgetary constraints can then turn the claimants into 'politicised symbolic entities' (Lockwood, 1996:541). So we see the two aspects of status identified by Marshal in play here, but note that in this example class position may be implicated in status position, though the legitimacy of the whole edifice is the notionally universal application of the rules – such that, at least in theory, anybody could share this fate.

However, Lockwood does observe that the dynamic of stigmatisation can be compounded by racial prejudice, especially notable since a lack of material resources and a disadvantaged class position will mean certain ethnic minorities are over-represented among welfare claimants (see Gov.uk, 2022). We could perhaps speak here of a discriminatory deficit, which extends to the treatment of minorities by a variety of public agencies, most notably the police, or in the case of migrants, the Home Office. The final form of deficit listed by Lockwood is fiscal deficit, which he says is best understood as the converse of fiscal gain (discussed below). However, he does mention *gastarbeiter* (guest workers) as likely victims of both stigmatisation and partial civic exclusion – and we can add to this the fiscal deficit some categories suffer, in paying taxes but being excluded from the full array of social rights. Most are also subject to a health surcharge in Britain, until they establish permanent residence (usually after five years, but sometimes ten).

Civic gain – Under this heading, Lockwood considers the way that formally equal entitlements can confer unequal benefits in that rights that can be exercised by all work substantially to the advantage of those with income, wealth, know-how and prestige. Prestige gain is the opposite of stigmatised deficit, and secures better treatment at the hands of authority according to perceived standing in society. It therefore combines the presence of rights with possession of moral and material resources, while power gain refers to the enhanced power to make use of rights, such as legal recourse as a remedy that often only the really wealthy can deploy. Fiscal gain refers mainly to tax relief attached to pension schemes, mortgages, investments, etc., which can notionally be claimed by all but in fact work in favour of those already in possession of significant material resources – and they attract less attention and disapprobation than does receipt of welfare benefits. Lockwood notes that while fiscal gains do favour the middle classes, there is sufficient cross-class benefit to prevent a politically significant division, though their legitimacy could be placed in contention in that fiscal gain serves as a multiplier of already established class advantage. While such gains are commonly justified in terms of reward for effort, they could equally be seen as a form of illegitimate inequality, but receive insufficient public exposure to prompt protest.

Civic expansion – Under the final form of civic stratification Lockwood considers the impulse to reach beyond the existing array of rights, such that citizenship has an inner logic that pushes at the outer limits imposed by scarcity and political constraints. Hence the frontiers of citizenship are 'continually tested and contested' (p.542), not least because those rights that do exist foster expectations of an ever greater degree of recognition and entitlement. This may take the form of demands for new rights, commonly pursued by civic activists who aspire not just to full citizenship but to an ever fuller citizenship. Lockwood gives examples such as environmental rights, universal human rights, freedom of information, the enlargement of civil liberties, etc. In such cases the absence of rights signalled in the '2 x 2' matrix refers to rights as yet to be 'invented' or established, and the role of civic activists is in part to build the moral resources through public education that will advance their various causes. However, the idea of civic expansion could also be applied where groups exist that do not hold the full array of rights – and perhaps those suffering extreme deficits – who seek to garner public support and accrue moral resources in order to push for either improved rights or fuller access to existing rights. In most cases these will be groups that lack not only the full array of rights but also the moral and material resources that would help their drive for expansion. Again, civic activists take a prominent role in building public support and enhanced moral standing for the groups concerned, and recourse to judicial review is a growing feature of both forms of expansion. Civic expansion therefore speaks to the question of how citizenship rights unfold over time, signalling the nature and form of struggle involved, despite the notion of an 'inner logic' of citizenship, or Marshall's 'urge forward' and 'continuous progression'.

Lockwood's elaboration of these four forms of civic stratification is an advance on Marshall in that it shows in some detail how rights can be the architect of inequality. However, the account he provides goes beyond the idea of legitimate inequality and in fact weighs more heavily on the side of illegitimate inequality, as exemplified by ascriptive exclusions, discriminatory and stigmatising deficits, and prestige gains. In so doing he problematises and politicises legitimacy, principally through the linkage between rights and moral resources, and the seeming negotiable nature of moral standing. There is already a hint in Marshall that beyond the narrow legal sense of status there is a social dimension to the conception of rights and duties, and to commonly valued behaviour, from which stems his view of citizenship as a form of recognition of social worth. This sense is also present in the idea of moral resources, or moral standing in society, and points to a terrain that clearly invites political manipulation or social intervention, as we see in the case of civic expansion.

However, Lockwood does not use this connection to consider that if rights can expand then perhaps they can also contract; if moral standing and the granting of rights are open to politicisation and social construction then there is no obvious basis for an assumption that they will always be driven by Marshall's 'urge forward' or Lockwood's 'inner logic'. But perhaps we do find in civic stratification some insight into Marshall's closing comments about the status differences that are creeping into citizenship, and his fear that conflicts within our social system are becoming too sharp. While Marshall does not dismiss the struggle that has been involved in establishing the rights of citizenship, Lockwood has given us some means of understanding the dynamic force at work in such struggle, its link to the moral standing of particular groups in society, and its socially constructed nature. The final stage of his article is to consider which forms of civic stratification are more or less likely to give rise to widespread and legitimate discontent. This addresses, at least in part, his question of 'under what conditions inequality is tolerated or rejected', while also having some bearing on Marshall's view that 'status differences can receive the stamp of legitimacy…provided that they do not cut too deep' (p.116).

Beginning with civic exclusion, Lockwood sees this as a common cause of disaffection in the past but as unlikely to generate major social conflict in the present, given the extension of civil and political rights, such that remaining anomalies are simply subject to piecemeal 'tidying-up measures' An exception to this, not apparent in Lockwood's lifetime, could be the Black Lives Matter movement, which took off in the US when the treatment of black people at the hands of the police seemed to amount to an exclusion from access to justice. In Britain, the scandal whereby denial of basic rights to some of the early arrivals from the Commonwealth (the Windrush generation) amounted to a civic exclusion, met with widespread public censure, but nevertheless fell some way short of provoking mass protest.

In fact, Lockwood does address ethnic discrimination under the heading of deficit, where he sees the deficits experienced by 'guest workers' and ethnic minorities as verging on exclusion and extending towards the second and third generation. This 'fault line' he considers as likely to widen, and he asks with some foresight 'why protest does not take on a more widespread political form' (p.544). He suggests some impediments to collective action, one being that minorities are themselves divided by class and by differing degrees of integration, which militate against collective action. Perhaps more telling is his argument that minority groups are 'caught up in the rules of the civic game' (p.544). They are therefore confronted by a choice between taking remedial action through the system or taking action outside the rules, which might itself increase prejudice and discrimination and even foster repression. But note the comments of Lawrence Tribe on the deployment of paramilitary federal forces against Black Lives Matter protesters in Portland: 'If ever there was a time for peaceful civil disobedience, that time is upon us' (Guardian, 2020).

With regard to other forms of deficit, Lockwood sees power deficit as the most potentially socially disruptive where there is a 'zero-sum' relation between the two parties – citing the 'paradigmatic' example of employer/employee relations, but also including women, minorities, and (with growing significance) children. Such cases, he says, are for the most part addressed by the creation of new ancillary rights intended to offset the power differential, but the limits of their success could be another aspect of deficit. The other two forms of deficit are viewed as even less likely to produce collective protest, with fiscal gains much better understood by those who receive them than those who do not. Hence, 'fiscal gain and loss is hardly at the forefront of public consciousness' and is remote from the 'everyday moral calculus' (p.546). This situation is somewhat changed since Lockwood's time of writing, since when the bailout for the banks in a period of growing public austerity, the inordinate profits of the fuel companies, the tax situation of large offshore companies have all been a focus for public concern and sometimes political mobilisation. Finally, stigmatised deficit, as in relation to welfare claimants, is deemed unlikely to generate protest as the group is neither a stagnant population nor homogeneous, being vertically divided according to the form of benefit at issue. Generally speaking, their moral and material resources are weak to begin with and 'further diminished by the indignity of the status itself' (p.546).

So Lockwood provides us with an analytical frame that goes beyond Marshall's model of citizenship as 'full membership' of society by revealing the ways in which citizenship itself can amount to a form of social stratification. Although Lockwood, like Marshall, refers to citizenship as legitimating certain forms of inequality – and he reiterates this in his concluding comments – his account of the four forms of civic stratification also serves to demonstrate that the operations of citizenship can generate types of inequality that are far from 'legitimate'. He gestures to the fact that legitimacy itself is constructed and contestable, being closely linked to socially elaborated and publicly sanctioned values that underpin the moral standing of any given social category.

We can now return to the questions yielded by a close reading of Marshall, and consider the ways in which Lockwood's work addresses and advances issues only partially explored or articulated by Marshall himself. On the relationship between citizenship and social class, Lockwood in effect reverses Marshall's problematic by asking not simply does citizenship serve to mitigate the inequalities of social class and render them acceptable when offset by this (notionally) uniform status, but rather how inequalities of class and status affect the institutionalisation of citizenship. Both Marshall and Lockwood take as their focus the relation between classes, defined by their economic position, and categories of citizen, defined through their access to rights and the classifications that govern their delivery. But rather than looking to how far citizenship status mitigates class inequality, Lockwood looks to how inequality can be written into citizenship. While accepting that the effects of social class are mediated by the rights of citizens, which are an additional factor to be taken into account in analyses of inequality, he argues that the practice of citizenship is 'heavily influenced by the structure of class and status' (p.547).

The effect of class is apparent in the various dynamics set out in the civic stratification matrix, and in the examples that Lockwood supplies, though he never specifically isolates the question of how and where class and citizenship merge in this sense. However, we can deduce that class operates in terms of deficit, through the power deficit experienced by employees vis-à-vis employers, and in the stigmatised deficit that affects some groups who are dependent on welfare, since vulnerability to unemployment is class-related, and is more severe among minority groups. Fiscal deficit is also class-related in that the stronger class locations are more likely to have access to civic gain, and similarly, prestige gain is class-related, as status and class are closely linked in advanced capitalist societies. So although Lockwood does not spell it out, citizenship can function as a multiplier of class advantage and disadvantage. Insofar as class differences are supported by a particular ideological frame, one which (as Lockwood points out) places a high value on individual achievement and self-responsibility, these class differences are legitimated and even amplified by the delivery and experience of citizenship rights.

However, that is not the only structured inequality that is apparent in the operation of citizenship and we have seen that in addition to these class-related differences the four forms of civic stratification are particularly revealing in relation to other (often ascriptive) bases of inequality, most notably race, gender, sexuality, age and migrant status. Although class may again play a part, these other sources of inequality are recurrent in relation to contemporary and historical exclusions, and the probability of deficits relating to power, discrimination, stigmatisation and fiscal status. These more ascriptive sources of inequality are also most likely to appear in expansionary movements to correct the deficits experienced, and as Lockwood observes, corrective movements are commonly advanced with the support, or on the initiative, of civic activists, often by seeking legal remedy through judicial review. The significance of activist intervention lies in part in lending the moral resources of established and respected organisations that work against poverty, gender discrimination, race discrimination, migrant exclusion, etc. The other aspect of the work of activists pushing for civic expansion is to raise public awareness, generate public sympathy and in so doing enhance the moral standing of disadvantaged groups. Hence, we arrive at Lockwood's concluding statement that: 'while its practice is heavily influenced by the structure of class and status inequality, citizenship can be seen to exert a forcefield of its own' (p.547).

Once the interweaving of class inequality and citizenship becomes apparent, then the question of the nature and limits of the compromise between the two becomes more complex, in that citizenship (as set out above) does not always work to ameliorate class disadvantage, or indeed disadvantage rooted in ascriptive categories. In fact, the limit of compromise is not a clear or static line but as Lockwood argues, is constantly tested and contested, most overtly in attempts at civic expansion, or indeed in contesting contraction – a process not remarked upon by Lockwood. So the limits of citizenship are under constant negotiation. As to whether the initial establishment and the fuller realisation of citizens' rights unfolds by an evolutionary urge forward, or by a process of struggle, again the outline forms of civic stratification are enlightening, especially civic expansion. But to refer back to Lockwood's '2 x 2' matrix and its paired oppositions of gain and deficit, exclusion and expansion, we should note that the opposite of exclusion is in fact inclusion, though that would render the matrix static. However, we might then pair expansion with contraction and so do fuller justice to the dynamic nature of citizenship; the limits of the urge forward or the inner logic of citizenship are then fought out in the legal and political arena, and while the original guarantees of citizenship have served to raise expectations and fuel expansion, the outcome should not be a foregone conclusion.

A central argument of Marshall's approach is that citizenship confers status equality through rights that are equally applicable to all members, while for Lockwood the governing system of uniform rules that oversee the delivery of rights secures legitimacy. What then of the status inequalities that run through civic stratification? We have seen that Marshall's double meaning of status applies to the legal standing conferred by citizenship and also the social value signalled by membership. However, in Lockwood's approach the sense of equal social worth notionally implied by full membership is disrupted not only by class but also by status dynamics. The conceptual tool for unpicking status differences is the notion of moral resources, so while citizenship signals social worth by virtue of full membership, access to and enjoyment of the accompanying rights is strongly affected by status. We see from Lockwood's four forms of civic stratification that this may occur through the prestige factors that enable civic gain, ascriptive features that fuel exclusion, and the stigmatisation or discrimination that produce deficits. Civic expansion then seeks to correct the flaws in the system by a struggle for status recognition and the accrual of moral resources – the latter sometimes achieved by building public sympathy or support, and other times by judicial intervention. So both the legal and social dimensions of status may be in play, but note that legal remedy to correct injustice may in some cases work against public sentiment, especially for issues that have been made a focus for political rhetoric (such as welfare dependency or immigration).

Now we can think again about the idea expressed by both Marshall and Lockwood that citizenship is the architect of legitimate inequality. The implication of this view is that where there is broad public consensus about social distinctions – such as differential wage rates, differential desert in relation to welfare, desirable and undesirable migrants, etc. they can be legitimately built into the delivery of citizenship rights 'provided [according to Marshall] that they do not cut too deep' ([1950] 1973:116). So 'legitimacy' becomes an object of social construction and ripe for political intervention, while the question of *when* differences cut too deep is a matter for interpretation. In Lockwood's model, it is moral resources that confer legitimacy, such that weak moral resources will often be linked to exclusion or deficit, while stronger moral resources could mean gain or the possibility of expansion. So this perhaps explains Marshall's fears that a stratified status system is creeping into citizenship, and that the conflicts in society are becoming too sharp – hence citizenship does not necessarily guarantee full membership (or we might say social inclusion), and forward progression is by no means certain.

What is missing from both Marshall's and Lockwood's approach is any discussion of the role of political rhetoric in shaping public sentiment in line with policy preferences. We have, however, seen that Marshall does recognise how individual rights can be superseded by national plans, while Lockwood is aware that a fiscal crisis of the state may constrain state action in the realm of rights. This is especially the case for social rights, where the 'fine-tuning' he mentions will rest upon particular political representations of claimants as either deserving or otherwise. So while the language of rights carries a sense of ethical certainty, in practice their granting and delivery is subject to political constraints, and to a legitimating process that can be strongly influenced by political rhetoric. In this context, citizenship as the architect of legitimate inequality takes on a much more political cast that fashions public sentiment in line with the content and delivery of rights, and legitimacy in line with national policy. As Marshall himself observes: 'What matters to the citizen is the superstructure of legitimate expectation' and 'the rate of progress depends on the magnitude of the national resources and their distribution between competing claims' (p.104). So legitimate expectation is subject to a process of social and political construction. Hence, as more contemporary writers observe (e.g. Munch, 2012), political rhetoric shapes the way problems are perceived and tackled, and the practice of rights thus occupies an uncertain and shifting terrain.

The concept of civic stratification and its four distinctive forms provide us with some tools for analysing the dynamic nature of rights and for placing their development more firmly in the context of struggle. That struggle can take place over the grounding of individual worth and moral resources, but inevitably raises further questions about the basis of moral standing in society. There are only hints in the work of Marshall and Lockwood, but contributing factors include public sentiment regarding particular social groups, as shaped by perceptions of their social worth. These perceptions are forcefully fashioned by political rhetoric but can also be influenced by campaigns conducted by those groups themselves or by civic activists who intervene on their behalf. The outcome cannot be predicted with any certainty, and while historically we can see that rights have expanded over time, the possibility of contraction is still quite strong, and the chapters to follow will provide some contemporary examples. The argument so far has suggested that the terrain of rights is an uncertain terrain, as Lockwood himself says, 'continually tested and contested' through a social and political dynamic that is never at rest but always in search of a negotiated balance between what the collective owes to the individual and what the individual owes to the collective.

References

Barbalet, J.M. (1988) *Citizenship,* Milton Keynes: Open University Press

Gov.uk (2022) State support - GOV.UK ethnicity facts and figures (ethnicity-facts -figures.service.gov.uk) (accessed 23.2.24)

The Guardian (2020) https://www.theguardian.com/us-news/2020/jul/20/trump-john -yoo-lawyer-torture-waterboarding 20 July (accessed 7.3.24)

Honneth, A. (1995) *The Struggle for Recognition,* Cambridge: Polity Press

Laenen, T., F. Rossetti, and W. Van Oorschot (2019) *Why Deservingness Theory Needs Qualitative Research,* SPSW Working Paper no. CeSo/SPSW/201901, Leuven: Centre for Sociological Research

Lockwood, D. (1974) 'For T.H. Marshall' *Sociology* 8(3):363–7

Lockwood, D. (1996) 'Civic integration and class formation' *British Journal of Sociology* 47(3):531–50

Mann, M. (1987) 'Ruling class strategies and citizenship' *Sociology* 21(3):339–54

Marshall, T.H. [1950] (1973) 'Citizenship and social class' in *Class, Citizenship and Social Development,* New York: Doubleday and Co., pp.65–122

Marshall, T.H. [1954] (1973a) 'A note on status' in *Class, Citizenship and Social Development,* New York: Doubleday and Co., pp.200–8

Marx, K. [1943] (1975) 'On the Jewish question' in *Karl Marx and Frederick Engels: Collected Works,* Volume 3, New York: International Publishers, pp.146–74

Munch, R. (2012) *Inclusion and Exclusion in the Liberal Competition State,* Abingdon: Routledge

Richardson, D. (1998) 'Sexuality and citizenship' *Sociology* 32(1), pp.83-100

Turners, B.S. (1986) *Citizenship and Capitalism,* London: Allen and Unwin

Walby, S. (1997) 'Is citizenship gendered' *Sociology* 28(2), pp.379-95

2 Welfare as social inclusion or stratified control?

Although Marshall's model of citizenship is built around the gradual unfolding of three sets of rights – civil, political and social – when it comes to the practical delivery of what Marshall ([1950] 1973:70) terms 'full membership' of society, then this seems to rest quite heavily on the 'social element'. Marshall recognised that civil and political rights had little direct effect on social inequality without an additional guarantee of

> the whole range from the right to a modicum of economic welfare and security to the right to share to the full in the social heritage and to live the life of a civilised being according to the standards prevailing in the society.
> (Marshall, [1950] 1973:72)

Yet Marshall's recognition of a possible conflict of principles (as noted in the previous chapter) is essentially a conflict between universal social guarantees and a competitive market economy. To be sure, his three sets of rights build incrementally towards the guaranteed inclusion he advocates, starting with those civil rights that secured the conditions for a transition from feudalism to a capitalist market economy. However, as Marshall observes, civil rights alone could be drawn on to justify the *denial* of social protection, in so far as each person was thereby equipped to compete and thus to provide for themselves. Conversely, he felt that political rights, together with civic freedoms, offered a means to fight for other rights, and social rights were then viewed by Marshall as the final stage in the delivery of full membership of society.

According to Marshall 'social rights imply an *absolute right* to a certain standard of civilisation that is conditional only on the discharge of the general duties of citizenship' (Marshall, [1950] 1973:94). As we will see, social rights can rarely (if ever) be viewed as absolute, and 'conditionality' has become an increasingly complex feature of welfare support, driving the erosion of social guarantees and their appropriation as a mode of control. However, in Marshall's model, social inclusion via citizenship rests on the delivery of certain guaranteed minimum standards – his 'absolutes'. It is not entirely clear how far Marshall was presenting a picture of a functioning model, based on

DOI: 10.4324/9781003324744-3

the history of British citizenship rights, and how far he was advocating an ideal towards which societies should strive, and his account seems to hover between these two different orientations. The same could be said of a shifting emphasis between the *status* equality enshrined in citizenship and the achievement of 'civilised' *material* standards.

With regard to the ideal picture of citizenship, Marshall [1950] (1973:84) observes that 'a society in which citizenship is developing creates an image of an ideal citizenship against which achievement can be measured and towards which aspiration can be directed'. This suggests that he is setting out a model that could in theory drive his 'urge forward towards a fuller measure of equality', but while equality of status takes a central role in this model, the concrete achievement of a minimum material standard also turns out to be pivotal. The transition from feudalism to market capitalism is depicted by Marshall as the invasion of status by contract, and the delivery of social rights 'in their modern form' as a reverse of this dynamic. They represent an invasion of contract by status, 'the subordination of market price to social justice and the replacement of free bargaining by the declaration of rights' (p.111), in effect creating a formal status group in the Weberian ([1922] 1948:183) sense. Status here refers to a group whose situation is not determined by market position, and who are guaranteed a real income that is not proportionate to their market value. Marshall's own emphasis was on a sense of status equality that attached to the position of all citizens, such that equality of status was more important than equality of income (Marshall, [1950] 1973:103). However, the status *distinction* between those who are and are not economically 'productive' has always threatened to undermine this vision.

Furthermore, while a key aspect of Marshall's argument is the claim that equality of status can override material inequalities (provided they do not cut too deep, p.116), in other respects he places considerable emphasis on material standards. Indeed, he sometimes moves on from what he first presents as a model to be aspired to and argues – with reference to the health system, for example – that 'the guaranteed minimum has been raised to such a height that the term "minimum"' becomes a misnomer' (p.104). Furthermore, his notion of loyalty to a civilisation which is a common possession (p.93), seems to be rooted quite firmly in the substantive achievement of 'a general enrichment of the concrete substance of civilized life and a general reduction of risk and insecurity' (p.102). Here, state-provided services, direct taxation and mass production of goods play a very significant role in his account of substantive movement towards the ideal, and Marshall's emphasis lies as much on existing progress towards a common *material* civilisation as on the equal *status* of citizens. At the very least, we can see that the two elements may be closely intertwined, such that the invasion of contract by status and the subordination of market price to social justice, must have real material implications to be meaningful.

For the equal status of citizens to be achieved in the manner set out by Marshall, all citizens must approximate his 'civilised' standard of living, but this of course begs a series of other questions. While Marshall recognises the potential conflicts or clash of principles entailed in his model, he hopes they might be containable by means of some strategic compromise, and hence, he looks to a unified civilisation established within the bounds of acceptable social inequalities. This is to be achieved through both parity of esteem and an acceptable standard of living secured for all, with basic rights contingent *only* on those duties 'most obviously and immediately necessary for the fulfilment of the right' (p.117). All have proved problematic in practice, as already signalled in Marx's [1844] (1975) most basic contention that rights delivered by the state cannot secure 'human emancipation' in a class-divided society. Nor can the class structure be changed by social rights based on redistribution, to the neglect of unequal structures of power and possessions, especially given an accompanying system of values whereby material success is itself a marker of prestige. In this context, the aim of a universal and equal status of citizenship immediately looks challenging, and the nature of that challenge is revealed by Marshall's own discussion of the meaning and sources of 'status'.

While Marshall sees status in the formal sense as a reference to 'legally established capacities and incapacities', he also sees a link to 'socially recognised rights and duties, and socially expected behaviour' (Marshall, [1954] 1973:205). So we can infer from this that seeing citizenship as a statement of equal social worth is only convincing if this view permeates established social perceptions. As Barbalet puts this: 'a status can be held only if it is publicly recognised as legitimate' and is therefore 'part of the fabric of society' (1988:16). Furthermore, status issues may flow over into the administration of rights – especially social rights – where judgements of desert can colour decision-making and implementation. Thus, Barbalet sees a service 'dominated by over-worked and under-staffed bureaucracies and professions...which tend to operate in ways that emphasise the dependent status of their clients' such that 'those most in need of social services are least likely to receive them as rights, properly understood' (p.66). These tendencies are inherent to the nature of social supports and are exacerbated by fiscal constraints at a higher level, which can filter down to ever more stringent requirements placed on the claimant (e.g. Guardian, 2023).

Lockwood's discussion of civic stratification provides us with a conceptual framework that helps both to analyse the dominant logic at work in the design and delivery of social rights and to explain something of how they are experienced. He pays particular attention to the basis of social integration in Marshall's model, to argue that this was not simply rooted in the equality of citizenship as a counterweight to class inequality, but also derived from a sense of community that flowed from 'loyalty to a civilisation which is a common possession' (Marshall, [1950] 1973:92). The achievement of this commonality was attributable in Marshall's account not just to 'sentiment and patriotism' but to 'material enjoyment' (p.96), such that mass production for the home market 'enabled the less well-to-do to enjoy a material civilisation which differed in quality less markedly from that of the rich' (p.96). But where Marshall also hopes for status equalisation to flow from citizenship guarantees, this is viewed as problematic by Lockwood, who notes: 'the broad-ranging distinction between the economically productive and state-dependent, between those in class situations and those in status situations, is bound to be a significant line of social differentiation in societies that are oriented to market values' (Lockwood, 1996:539). In other words, the equalising role of citizenship as a common status – particularly in its social dimension – is hard to sustain when status judgements are closely tied to material success, and as Sayer has argued (2005), class is a strong determinant of social standing (i.e. status) in contemporary capitalist society.

As we have seen, this tension is recognised by Marshall, but his emphasis is on the role of citizenship in supporting a claim to be admitted to a share in the social heritage, as marked by the standard of civilised life. In reversing the focus of Marshall's model, Lockwood emphasises the differentiating force of citizenship when exposed to values driven by market competition. Thus, he argues that since equality of civil and political rights is itself 'constitutive of capitalist liberal democracy' (p.535), the contradiction between citizenship and capital has come to turn on the negotiable nature of a commitment to social rights, particularly in the context of a fiscal crisis of the state. The result is a shifting balance between what Lockwood (1996:533–4) terms 'system integration', which refers to the viability and cohesion of the whole socio-economic edifice, and 'social integration', which refers to the incorporation of all citizens into what Marshall would term the 'social heritage'. However, it is the guarantee of civilised standards of living that has most often been deemed expendable, and so accordingly welfare issues have received the most extensive treatment in Lockwood's elaboration of civic stratification and its four forms (outlined in the previous chapter).

Blanket formal *exclusion* from social rights is now rare within the category of citizenship, though the exclusion of non-citizens from welfare entitlement has increasingly been a focus for activist intervention, and this is documented in the chapter to follow. However, for full citizens, exclusions can still occur under the terms and conditions of entitlement, which can impose variable reporting and behavioural requirements, financial sanctions for failure to meet such conditions, and differential rates of support for different social categories. While *ascriptive* exclusions with respect to race or gender have been formally discredited, they are still detectable through patterns of disadvantage or bias in the way a welfare system operates, but are perhaps more appropriately viewed as stigmatised or discriminatory *deficits*. In practice, the legitimating argument cited by Lockwood – that the system operates by the application of impersonal rules such that any citizen may share the same fate – loses its purchase when evidence points to recurrent vulnerabilities of class, race and gender (see for example the Women's Budget Group, 2017). While *civic gain* refers to the preferential or deferential treatment received by the wealthy in their dealings with officialdom, its converse, civic deficit, follows patterns of class disadvantage that are also mediated by gender and race.

The deficits experienced by welfare claimants stem precisely from the fact that they are in a status-determined situation such that, in Lockwood's (1996:538) words, 'the structure and operation of social citizenship…of its own accord creates incipient status groups of a negatively privileged kind'. The stratified nature of civic status is thus simply expressed as a reversal of Marshall's hoped-for effects, and as a system that 'legitimates the allocation of inferior resources to claimants but also has the effect of reconstituting them as second class citizens' (Lockwood, 1996:538). Hence the status-determined situation of welfare claimants constitutes them as lesser citizens, whose position marks them out as failures and potential frauds, whose lives must be open to close inspection and whose very circumstances deprive them of the 'moral resources' needed to press for fuller recognition and for an expansion of rights. Their relation to the state, in Lockwood's view, is that of passive recipients, 'objects of surveillance (who are) publicly singled out as lacking in civic virtue' (p.539), and this is sometimes reflected by their treatment at the hands of those who administer the service. Thus, Lockwood argues (p.540) that large numbers of citizens who are dependent on state welfare then acquire their distinct collective identities by virtue of their classification into categories of lesser 'moral worth'. This in turn rebounds on any prospect of *civic expansion* through the mobilisation of moral resources and appeal to a sympathetic public, though it is here that activist groups can sometimes step in and lend their own moral standing to a cause.

The case of social rights, and particularly the functioning of the welfare system, thus gives perhaps the clearest illustration of civic stratification in operation – stratification here referring to the creation of a dependent category of lesser citizens. Instead of the guarantee of a civilised standard of living that Marshall hoped for, we have (according to Lockwood) a system that legitimates the application of lower standards and operates through built-in mechanisms of surveillance and control. In fact, the stratified effects go much further, as the system itself subdivides claimants into what Lockwood (1996:540) terms 'several public identities' who: 'by virtue of their removal or exclusion from relations of production…are immediately reconstituted by their relations to the means of social security, and thereby classified into categories of different moral worth'. Indeed, they are made subject to differential requirements that have themselves been the focus of considerable scholarly attention. Much of this work points to varying conditions of entitlement and associated status rankings within the broader category of benefit receipt, as elaborated by Clasen and Clegg (2007). These writers argue that *categories* of inclusion and exclusion (e.g. unemployment, disability, old age), *circumstances* of eligibility (e.g. nature and extent of disability, household size and structure) and requirements of *conduct* (as enforced by official conditions) differentially affect entitlement for a variety of claimant groups.

In fact, 'deservingness theory' all but amounts to a distinctive sub-field in social policy research, and a dominant approach (see Van Oorschot et al, 2017) argues that public support for welfare provision turns upon the application of five key criteria – the so-called 'CARIN-criteria' – that shape views on what constitutes a fair distribution of social resources. These criteria are labelled control, attitude, reciprocity, identity and need – though it is also recognised (Laenen, Rossetti and Van Oorschot, 2019) that the concrete substance of such essentially abstract indicators is not self-evident but requires interpretation. Their meaning can be summarised as follows:

> the amount of control and therefore responsibility that claimants have over their situation, their attitude in terms of willingness to assume responsibility, their general contribution to the system, their position in relation to 'belongingness', and their level of material need.
>
> (Morris, 2021:99)

It has also been shown (Meuleman et al., 2020) that judgments of 'deservingness' serve as a mediator between social structural position and associated policy preferences, with some social groups more likely to support particular logics of desert than others. So, for example, lower socio-economic groups who are most likely to depend on welfare support are also more likely to judge desert in a restrictive manner.

Broadly speaking, a ranking of claimant groups in terms of the public sympathy they evoke has commonly moved from the elderly, to the sick and disabled, the unemployed and finally to immigrants (Van Oorschot, 2008; Meuleman et al., 2020) – and we might add lone parents to this list, at around the mid-point. However, there is also room for variable treatment of claimants even within these categories, based for example on duration of unemployment, degrees of sickness or disability, the age of the youngest child for lone parents, how long the elderly have paid into National Insurance schemes, etc. Furthermore, perceptions of each of these criteria and their hierarchical ordering are open to change, manipulation and negotiation, while Laenen et al. (2019) report the existence of an 'institutional logic' in popular welfare preferences. They argue that respondents will tend to echo the normative criteria that are most strongly embedded in the institutional structure of their own country's welfare regime. Thus, they find that 'financial need was the guiding criterion in 'liberal' UK, and reciprocity was dominant in 'corporatist-conservative' Germany (while) in 'social democratic' Denmark, it proved impossible to single out one dominant normative criterion' (Laenen et al., 2019:1). However, any such classification will, by its nature, be as unstable as the economic and political context in which it operates.

In fact, the boundaries of classification deployed within any given system can shift over time and are not simple reflections of public sentiment, in that such sentiment can be actively constructed by political interests and a supporting rhetoric that seeks to influence wider perceptions. Hence the argument from Munch (2012) that political rhetoric shapes the way policy problems are perceived and tackled; a view that reflects concerns previously addressed by Mary Douglas (1986) in her work on 'how institutions think'. She notes that institutionalised systems of classification are central to the way in which social life is organised, such that institutions 'think' – or perhaps we should say carry meaning – through the distinctions that underpin their administrative procedures, which in turn can shape public opinion. So Douglas (1986:99) asks: 'how can we possibly think of ourselves in society except by using the classifications established in our institutions'. This kind of argument directs attention away from public perceptions *per se*, and towards the deployment of political rhetoric and the policy shifts it supports, also feeding into the public recognition that Marshall and others see as underpinning the legitimacy of distinctive rights claims (Marshall, [1954] 1973:205; Barbalet, 1988:16).

My own work (Morris, 2021) has pointed to a reframing of the concept of 'moral economy' as one approach to analysing this dynamic. This concept was initially adopted by E.P. Thompson (1971) with reference to popular protests against rising prices that emerged in 18th century Britain, and their demand for moral accountability on the part of feudal landowners. While Thompson's account of this phenomenon speaks of 'the moral economy of the poor', and can in this sense be construed as 'moral economy from below', a number of writers (Booth, 1994; Fassin, 2009; Sayer, 2007; Clarke and Newman, 2012) have reversed the dynamic. In so doing they make an argument most clearly expressed by Booth (1994:662), that 'all economies…are moral economies, embedded in the (ethical) framework of their communities', thus pointing to the role of the economy in the 'architecture' of community (p.663). The advantage of this construal lies in drawing attention to the moral sentiments informing policy, the ideological positions that shape claims to legitimacy, the associated framing of notions of desert, and the constructed and possibly changeable nature of public sentiment. We can then make a connection to Lockwood's model of civic stratification, in that the presence or absence of moral resources for a particular group will be affected by public perceptions of their circumstances and desert.

Against this background, it may be instructive to follow through on the centrality of social rights in Marshall's British-based model of citizenship and to consider the way welfare provisions have developed in the UK since his time of writing. In the course of the post-war period, and since the publication of his famous essay, we find policy shifts that heighten the conditions built into welfare entitlement, and their increased deployment in attempts to control the behaviour of claimants. This in turn enshrines particular conceptions of desert in policy measures, which then reflect and possibly erode the moral standing of the claimants groups affected. As Harris (2008:49) puts it in tracing this history: 'The idea that employment is a personal responsibility…[is] part of the managerialistic governance of welfare that places an emphasis on strict controls with contractual underpinnings'.

Hence, an account of the history of social welfare provision in Britain shows both continuity and mounting intensification in the underlying policy rationale, driven by ever-present suspicions of abuse and an assumed need to enforce self-reliance through work, supported by financial penalties for failure to comply with official direction. Marshall's ideal of an absolute guarantee of support that is 'conditional only on the discharge of the general duties of citizenship' soon begins to crumble, to be replaced by Lockwood's stratified citizenship status and the associated notion of the second class citizen. Harris (2008) has traced a basic continuity in British social security law since 1911 onwards, evident in two main areas: requirements related to job search, and financial penalties for non-compliance. These have been played out in an increasingly complex system of classification and boundary drawing that casts its net ever wider, from the involuntarily unemployed, to those with 'limited capacity for work',[1] and to lone parents of ever younger children.

A period of intensification was most markedly apparent in the course of the austerity decade, announced by the incoming Prime Minister David Cameron in 2009, and implemented by two pieces of legislation that were designed to carry through his 'moral mission' of welfare reform (Cameron, 2012) – the 2012 Welfare Reform Act, and the 2016 Welfare Reform and Work Act. The measures that these acts put into place consolidated and intensified devices of control that were already in operation, expanding the classification of claimant groups and its attendant 'conditionality' regime. They went further than previous measures in a number of ways, not least by incorporating both out-of-work support and supplements for the low-paid within an integrated system of Universal Credit, thus extending the reach of conditionality (Guardian, 2016). The increasing complexity of the system eats away at the promise of equal standing for all citizens, such that claimants share a common negative status of 'dependency' while also being sub-divided by the conditions that attach to their benefit. The associated mechanisms of control then carry with them varied forms of implied condemnation, with each claimant group subject in its own way to judgements of inadequacy, censure or blame that both inform their treatment and shape their perception in the public gaze. In Lockwood's words, they bear 'a mark of inferiority…are treated as potential frauds, subject to the discretionary powers of state officials, and have their

---

1 At the time of writing, the abolition of the Work Capability Assessment was under consideration, to be replaced by an individual work coach approach, though conditionality also seems likely to increase (see Guardian 2023a; 2024)

lives open to close inspection' (p.538), all of which serves to erode their moral standing (see Guardian, 2023, 2024).

The circular process in operation first defines the group and its claimed characteristics, then constructs a corrective intervention as dictated and legitimised by those determining features, and finally confirms the group's existence in the eyes of the public by virtue of its administrative designation. The expanding classification of claimant groups subject to 'conditionality' (Welfare Conditionality Project, 2018) encompasses the unemployed, with differing degrees of control according to duration; the long-term sick or disabled, with disciplinary controls for those with a 'limited capacity for work'; lone parents with a youngest child under 3 – this age having been reduced in graduated steps from 12 in 2008 (Millar, 2018); and the low-paid in receipt of supplements to their wage, now construed as a newly emergent problem of 'entrenched dependency' (Department of Work and Pensions (DWP), 2010). The application of 'sanctions' was heightened under the declared period of 'austerity' and takes the form of deductions from benefits for failure to meet the conditions of a claim, thus conveying a conferral of blame and asserting the moral legitimacy of the system. The stratified system was also further elaborated by the introduction of a 'benefit cap' that places a limit on the total amount of benefit that a household can receive (first in 2012 then lowered in 2016)[2] regardless of family size, and a two-child limit for receipt of child tax credits.

All of these measures have the same driving rationale, the 'rhetoric' which in Munch's terms shapes the way problems are perceived and tackled, and which points to one aspect of the dynamic nature of rights. Thus, the period of austerity was ushered in by assertions such as: 'if you refuse to work we will not let you live off the hard work of others' (Cameron, 2010), and allegations (from Iain Duncan Smith) of a 'something for nothing culture' (Guardian, 2013) that would be diminished by a more robust system of conditions and sanctions. So benefit rates were frozen, job search requirements for the unemployed were set at 35 hours per week, and the longest possible sanction was raised from 26 weeks to 3 years (the latter was eventually to be abolished after widespread criticism). The same rationale extended to the 'Work Related Activity Group' (WRAG) made up of the sick and disabled deemed to have 'a limited capacity for work'. Membership of this category was to be determined by a tougher and highly controversial Work Capability Assessment (WCA), with discipline enforced by cuts and stronger sanctions (Kennedy et al., 2016). The groups also saw the removal of an additional support supplement of £30 per week, intended to address 'the financial incentive that would

---

2 The cap was originally set at £26,000 pa for couples and lone parents. From 2016 it was lowered and two rates were applied, one London based at £23,000 pa and one for outside London at £20,000 pa. They were raised to £25,323 pa and £22,020 pa respectively in 2023.

otherwise discourage claimants from taking steps back to work'. (Murphy and Keen, 2016). Abolition of the WCA has since come under consideration, but with pressure on disabled claimants to find work, including working from home, set to increase (Financial Times, 2023; Guardian, 2023a)[3]

Lone parents have also been a group subject to greater scrutiny under 'austerity' measures, with the lowering of the age of the youngest child to three for determining the point at which lone parents can be subject to work-seeking requirements, despite the inadequacy of funded childcare provision (Guardian, 2024a). The 'benefit cap' was a further 'work incentive' measure and has (perversely) had a major impact on lone parents – in capping total household benefit income with reference to the 'average family wage' it omitted the benefits available to such families from the calculation. Even this rationale was later undermined when the cap was further reduced and it was revealed that a large majority of those affected were not required to be actively seeking work (Work and Pensions Committee, 2019), and that benefits paid on behalf of children were included in the calculation (Child Poverty Action Group (CPAG), 2014). Equally contentious has been the two-child limit on receipt of Child Tax Credits, intended to ensure that claimants 'face the same financial choices about having children as those supporting themselves solely through work' (HM Treasury, 2015: para 1.145). Both the two-child limit and the benefit cap have been criticised as detracting from payments made on behalf of a child in order to motivate the parents to find work (see CPAG, 2014; Kennedy at al., 2017) and in this sense they extend civic stratification to the differential treatment of citizen children.

All of the measures introduced in the 'austerity' decade were launched under a supporting rhetoric of fairness to the hard-working taxpayer (e.g. Cameron, 2012), presenting dependency as a behavioural choice that is underpinned by a distinctive cultural orientation, and which can be amended by disciplinary correction (Adler, 2016). These sentiments have been repeated more recently in Chancellor Jeremy Hunt's statement that: 'anyone choosing to coast on the hard work of taxpayers will lose their benefits' (Guardian, 2023). The role of such rhetoric in shaping sentiment is of particular interest with respect to civic stratification in that the rationale of the measures directed at distinctive claimant groups informs the relevant policy design, but more significantly is conveyed to the public as a legitimising rationale. It operates by claiming a principle capable of broad endorsement – such as 'fairness' or 'morality' – and proceeding to give it a particular material content such that, as Freeden (1996, 2003) argues, 'social truths' are made to turn upon the translation of abstract concepts into substantive meaning. Political ideology is viewed in this context as a recurrent pattern of beliefs and values dedicated to (re)ordering the social world, and an appreciation of this process can therefore advance our understanding and analysis of civic stratification.

---

3 A general election is pending at the time of writing

In the *formal* sense of civic stratification, the political rhetoric and its under-pinning rationale provide the basis for the regulatory rules and procedures that govern access to social rights, but in terms of the *informal* dimension, it can erode or enhance the moral standing of the claimant groups in question. In Lockwood's model (1996:536), the dynamic nature of rights derives from the fact that citizenship 'remains an ideal whose actualisation is always less than complete', and in the drive for its fuller realisation through *civic expansion* campaigners will draw upon the moral and material resources at their disposal. Where groups carry with them reserves of public sympathy then the prospects of expansion are greatly enhanced, but what of the converse possibility? We have seen how Lockwood's model operates through two paired oppositions – civic gain and civic deficit, and civic expansion and civic exclusion. However, if we set exclusion against the more obvious opposite of inclusion, as argued by Bechofer (1996) and outlined in the previous chapter, this opens up the pos-sibility of a third opposition – expansion and contraction. At this point, we can think back to the concept of moral economy, and more specifically the argu-ment that 'all economies are moral economies' to think about how in Douglas's (1986) terms, social judgements come ready prepared by our own institutions.

The judgements at issue relate to fairness, dependency and responsibility, which together underpin what Harris (2008) termed 'the managerialistic gov-ernance of welfare' whereby benefit dependence bespeaks a lack of responsi-ble behaviour, which is in turn deemed unfair to the 'hardworking taxpayer' (e.g. Cameron, 2009, 2010; London Broadcasting Company (LBC), 2023). The stated aim of devices for surveillance and control that pervade the system is to enforce behavioural change by 'incentivising' employment (Kennedy, 2015; Gov.uk, 2023) and making life on benefits less viable as a means of sur-vival. Philip Alston (2018:3), the UN Special Rapporteur on extreme poverty and human rights, summed up this effect as follows:

> It is the underlying values and ethos shaping the design and implementa-tion of specific measures that have generated the greatest problems…it is the mentality that has informed many of the reforms that has brought the most misery and wrought the most harm to the fabric of British society.

Sanctions in particular are singled out as 'instilling a fear and loathing of the system in many claimants' (p.6), but Alston argues more generally that the whole system applies discipline where it is of least use, imposes a rigid order on the lives of vulnerable people, and elevates blind compliance over concern for well-being. Here he is implicitly raising the question of 'agency', that is the extent to which disciplinary measures assume that people could behave differently, that they have brought their problems upon themselves, and that they can be coerced or cajoled into 'behavioural change'.

The underlying issue concerns the assumed explanation for unemploy-ment and poverty, and whether people are wilfully avoiding work – so, for example, assuming that appropriate work is in fact available for the unemployed, that affordable and viable childcare services exist for lone parents, or that the sick or disabled are in fact fit enough to work, etc. Human agency has traditionally been construed in terms of purposive 'rational' action – that is action (rather than behaviour) consciously chosen with a specific end in mind – and where there is purpose there is also the possibility of blame. Thus Wright (2012) argues that welfare policies that aim at behavioural change operate with assumptions about individual choice and thus of culpability and accountability that then provide the justification for 'conditionality' and sanctions. Such assumptions therefore carry a moral burden in attributing responsibility to welfare claimants for 'behaviour' that is deemed unacceptable, thus engaging the model of civic stratification by virtue of what is effectively an assault on moral standing and public credibility. However, a number of writers (Emirbayer and Mische, 1998; Sayer, 2011) have argued there is more to agency than rational purpose, and that 'actors' are embodied beings, located in nested and overlapping relationships of care and concern, and rooted in plans and experiences that extend from past to future obligations. Actions, options and decisions must therefore be understood in this context, and are arguably better approached through Sayer's (2011) notion of 'practical reason' rather than through a disembodied, non-contextual construal of 'rational choice'.

This at the very least means that action must be understood within the contours of a setting that is relevant to, and possibly constraining for, the actor – and which once understood could restore their moral integrity. So as rules change or intensify over time, they will also rebound on popular representations of claimant groups, and increasingly amount to a terrain of active intervention – both by policy makers and by interested parties who might seek to question dominant construals of motivation and choice. It is commonly argued that an ideological position, when offered as a particular characterisation of the social world, cannot be challenged by empirical fact, but it is nevertheless possible for the claims of a stated position to be evaluated in their own terms. So here we can turn the lens of rationality away from claimant behaviour to examine the assumptions that inform the purpose and design of policy itself. For example, a quest for behavioural change, to be enforced by the regulations and requirements governing entitlement to benefits, must first ensure that the subjects have full awareness and comprehension of the rules themselves.

An early review of the Jobseeker's Allowance sanctions scheme (Oakley, 2014) found that claimants from more vulnerable groups lacked a clear understanding of the requirements that were placed on them, and one prime provider reported one in three clients had health issues, mental health problems or a learning disability. A key finding of the report was therefore that poor communication could render the aim of behavioural change ineffective, and this conclusion received support from a legal challenge to the imposition of sanctions. Two claimants who had been less than fully informed about the schemes in operation, and additionally had been given no written notice of the sanction or had been given inadequate details, successfully challenged the imposition of a penalty (Reilly and Wilson v Secretary of State for Work and Pensions (SSWP) [2013] United Kingdom Supreme Court (UKSC) 68). So rationality issues here tip over into questions of legality, and a similar argument can be made in relation to a successful challenge to the Work Capability Assessment (CJ and SG v SSWP [2017] United Kingdom Upper Tribunal (UKUT) 0324) that raised questions of what might be termed embodied agency. The purpose of this test was to determine the appropriate requirements to be placed on a claimant but was ruled to have unlawfully discriminated against people with mental health problems, who had difficulties understanding and negotiating the test itself.

Other examples include the faulty design of the benefit cap (CPAG, 2014), and the claim that a differential between average earnings and income from benefit was necessary as a work incentive when such a differential already existed before the imposition of the cap. Also, the group most strongly affected by the cap are lone parents, and here caring obligations must be factored in, especially since a large majority of capped claimants were anyway not required to seek employment – issues which have been raised in several legal challenges (see Morris, 2020). A further example of constrained agency has recently been raised by the extension of conditionality to low-paid/part-time workers (Guardian, 2016). When required to increase their hours of work or suffer cuts to their benefits, some of those affected 'struggle to increase their hours because of health issues, childcare and other constraints' – constraints which include the complexity of many claimants' lives.

In terms of civic stratification, the point at issue in such cases is not so much the pursuit of civic expansion, but how to contest and arrest *contraction*. One associated question is how far arguments of this kind could correct the erosion of moral standing entailed in the political discourse promoting policy change, and also in the design and implementation of the measures themselves. Here argument goes beyond rationality and legality to engage more directly with morality itself, which implicitly addresses Lockwood's (1996:231) opening question – 'under which conditions inequality is tolerated or rejected'. Many commentaries on the austerity years in Britain point to the failure to secure anything like Marshall's 'life of a civilised being', and at the extreme we find accounts of starvation following on from flaws in the benefits system (Guardian, 2020, 2014), women engaging in survival sex to feed their families (Work and Pensions Committee, 2019a) and a link between welfare cuts and rising cases of suicide.

Many organisations have expressed a repeated sentiment – that 'the social safety net is failing in its basic duty to ensure that families have access to sufficient income to feed themselves adequately' (Church Action on Poverty (CAP)/Oxfam, 2013), a moral condemnation that is strengthened by reference to Britain's position as the world's seventh largest economy (End Hunger, 2014). The Joseph Rowntree Foundation, in their annual Minimum

Income Standard report (Guardian, 2022) found that among households reliant on benefits, a single working-age adult would achieve only 32% of the minimum needed for a decent standard of living, and a lone parent with two children would achieve 52%. The organisation therefore calls for a reform of the welfare system, in terms of public perceptions of what is required to live in *dignity,* a concept whose use in this setting calls to mind not simply the guarantees of citizenship but rather the underlying principle of universal human rights (as expressed in the preamble to the Universal Declaration of Human Rights (UDHR)). This brings an extra dimension to thinking about civic stratification.

Lockwood's interest in civic stratification stems from an awareness that the 'universality' of Marshall's citizenship model (albeit confined to citizens) was universal only in the sense that the same rules applied to all. It was not universal in its actual effects, and especially not in the case of the welfare guarantees, which offer to the state the greatest scope for adjusting rights with respect to other priorities. Yet in the British case this 'fine-tuning' has gone so far as to prompt an approach to social rights that looks beyond citizenship guarantees to the force of international law in asserting the principles associated with universal human rights. In fact, even human rights guarantees fall short of full universality, in part because those rights that are secured by fully ratified international conventions can contain within them absolute, limited and qualified rights. The latter are open to qualifying conditions or requirements, which may make reference to national security, public safety or the economic well-being of the country, while even absolute rights require interpretation. In fact, social rights are the least firmly justiciable rights in the context of international human rights law, but some important developments have nevertheless occurred, and where a national government fails to secure minimum standards of living for its citizens, those citizens have sometimes looked to international courts for a remedy.

When Hannah Arendt ([1948] 1979) famously wrote of the relationship between citizenship and human rights, she argued that 'the right to have rights' depends upon a status of belonging within some form of rights-granting community which then has a duty to honour the claim to a variety of contingent rights. This is why Arendt concluded that, in the absence of a legal and political community to adjudicate universal claims, the loss of citizenship was tantamount to a loss of human rights altogether. She was writing just before the launching of the UDHR, and also looking back to the Declaration of the Rights of Man, but reflecting on the period after the First World War and the dilemma faced by stateless people in its aftermath. We will come back to her argument in the chapter to follow, but should note here that the situation is now somewhat changed in that citizens increasingly look to human rights in seeking to assert the guarantees that Marshall took to be the hallmark of citizenship. So when it comes to civic stratification we can ask how far the legal and moral force of universal human rights law and principles can be called on to limit the erosion of citizenship rights, and/or advance the 'urge forward' to an ever fuller array of rights.

Where a contraction of rights has been preceded by the denigration of affected claimant groups, such that they are held responsible for their own problems, and lose public support or sympathy in the process, there is still scope for challenge and contestation. The possibility of collective action by the claimants themselves is in Lockwood's (1996:546) terms diminished by their internal sub-divisions, and by 'the indignity of the status', but their cause may be taken up in public campaigning and/or legal action by what Lockwood terms 'civic activists'. While activist intervention may seek to restore the moral standing of groups placed under the discipline, scrutiny and surveillance of the welfare system, Lockwood notes that 'recourse to judicial review of legislation is a more and more frequent feature' (p.543). Indeed, when Alston (2018:7) points to 'the gradual disappearance of the postwar British welfare state behind a webpage and an algorithm' he also states that 'the impact on the human rights of the most vulnerable will be immense'.

Despite Marshall's view that 'social rights imply an *absolute right*' conditional only on the general duties of citizenship, there is no such straightforward guarantee in either citizens' rights or human rights law. The UDHR and the ICESCR (International Covenant on Economic Social and Cultural Rights) both embrace the right to an adequate standard of living, but the former is not justiciable, while the latter Covenant (in article 2) simply requires signatory states to 'take steps…to the maximum of its available resources, with a view to achieving progressively the full realisation of the rights recognized'. There is a strong presumption against retrogression, which must be justified by reference to the totality of rights and full use of available resources (Committee on Economic Social and Cultural Rights (CESCR), 1990), but this leaves considerable scope for interpretation. There is, however, a non-discrimination requirement under the ICESCR, and in article 14 of the European Convention on Human Rights (and therefore the Human Rights Act (HRA)), which is also enforced in Britain by the Equalities Act (2010). In fact, discrimination has featured among some of the strongest challenges to the impact of austerity measures in relation to gender, race and disability, and it is the discriminatory impact of measures on the enjoyment of other rights that has produced some of the most effective legal argument.

A number of legal challenges in Britain have therefore tested out how far the guarantees of universal human rights law can arrest the erosion of welfare guarantees that have been a feature of the austerity agenda. So where citizenship guarantees fail, do universal human rights place a limit on how far civic stratification can go in advancing an unequal citizenship, thus marking the point beyond which inequality is not to be tolerated? As suggested above, the purchase of human rights has not been through the direct assertion of a right to support – and one argument (Reilly and Wilson v SSWP [2013] UKSC 68) that compulsory unpaid work as a condition for welfare amounted to forced labour was firmly rejected. Nor do guaranteed minimum standards *per se* have much force, but human rights law has been brought to bear more effectively where discrimination or various administrative failings have affected the enjoyment of other rights. These have included the peaceful enjoyment of possessions (article 1, protocol 1 (A1P1) of the Economic Convention on Human Rights (ECHR)), which has been ruled to apply to welfare benefits (STEC and Ors v United Kingdom, GC 2005); the right to family life (article 8 of the ECHR); or access to justice (article 6 of the ECHR). So when the DWP retrospectively corrected and validated flawed regulations that had been the basis of an appeal against a sanction, this was deemed a denial of the right to a fair hearing for the claimant.

The negative impact of the benefit cap has been at issue in several challenges, firstly in a case involving gender discrimination in relation to A1P1, when it was also viewed as a possible breach of the Convention of the Rights of the Child (CRC). There was a considerable range of opinion among the five judges (SG and Ors v SSWP [2015] UKSC 16) but a majority ruled against gender discrimination, or saw it as justified by the legitimate aims of the measure, while the CRC had no direct force as it had not been incorporated into domestic law. A further challenge against the cap (DA and Ors v SSWP [2019] UKSC 21) arguing discrimination in relation to lone parents with a child under two, dropping the gender dimension but engaging A1P1, and potentially the right to family life, also failed. The families at issue were deemed insufficiently distinct as to amount to a clearly designated 'other status' for the purposes of discrimination (DA, DS and Ors v SSWP [2019] UKSC 21). However, judges in both cases expressed severe misgivings about the impact on children, especially in relation to the CRC. One further case (Hurley and Ors v SSWP [2015] England and Wales High Court (EWHC) 3382) based on the discriminatory impact of the cap did succeed, however, in relation to A1P1 for the carer, and in relation to article 8 of the ECHR (private and family life) for disabled people, by virtue of the non-exemption from the cap for households in receipt of carers allowance.

These are some examples of ongoing challenges to the curtailment of welfare rights, and though falling short of complete success they have served to give an airing to issues of considerable legal and public interest. They are not completely without effect, but they do demonstrate the difficulties of holding domestic legislation to established human rights principles in relation to a guaranteed minimum standard of living – and they also point to the growing complexity of civic stratification with respect to effective social rights. The need and desire for some forum of adjudication on established standards, outside the arena of domestic politics, has become more pressing and it is of great significance that claimants and activists have increasingly looked to universal human rights for a remedy.

It is also interesting to note that some writers have pointed to the need for a fourth phase in Marshall's history of the unfolding development of rights, a phase above and beyond the national focus of citizenship rights, and extending to the realm of universals. This then would seem to strengthen the validity of Lockwood's reversal of Marshall's analysis, to focus on the inequalities built into the functioning of citizenship. We have already noted his concluding argument (Lockwood, 1996:547) that 'while its practice is heavily influenced by the structure of class and status inequality, citizenship can be seen to exert a forcefield of its own'. One aspect of that 'forcefield' is argued to lie in the legitimation of inequality, but though this point is also made by Marshall it is not fully developed by either writer and its meaning is not entirely clear. In Marshall's case, it refers to the opening up of opportunities across the class structure such that individuals were no longer tied at birth to a class position they held throughout life. This does not seem to be the focus of Lockwood's own remark, and indeed the consolidation of class position through grossly unequal chances of upward mobility remains strongly entrenched (Bukodi et al., 2015). However, what we can say with respect to the unfolding of the welfare reforms of the austerity years is that patterns of grossly unequal citizenship rights *have* been legitimised by a highly questionable 'moral message' that has tested to its extreme the extent to which inequality is tolerated or rejected.

Under these conditions, a claim to rights may require recourse to what Arendt [1948] (1979) felt to be lacking at her own time of writing – a legal and political community outside the nation state that can adjudicate such claims, and as such could bring legitimacy to challenges that contest the acceptability of contraction. For Arendt, possession of citizenship provided the ultimate guarantee, as it did for Marshall, but when citizenship itself fails to deliver there needs to be another means of calling national governments to account. This is the space that is filled by the promise of universals – the basic rights that should be a taken-for-granted underpinning of social and political existence, and that could place a limit on the extremes of civic stratification. However, while citizens increasingly look to universal human rights to shore up what they might expect from their own governments, Marshall's [1950] (1973:116) conception of citizenship as a 'universal' status begs some further pressing questions – how are the boundaries of the national community drawn, who is excluded from belonging, and how. These are questions that the notion of civic stratification is well placed to answer, as we see in the chapter to follow.

References

Adler, M. (2016) 'A new Leviathan' *Journal of Law and Society* 43(2):195–227

Alston, P. (2018) *Statement on Visit to the United Kingdom,* United Nations Special Rapporteur on Extreme Poverty and Human Rights, Office of the High Commissioner   https://www.ohchr.org/en/NewsEvents/Pages/DisplayNews.aspx?NewsID=23881&LangID=E 16 November (accessed 24.2.24)

Arendt, H. [1948] (1979) *The Origins of Totalitarianism,* New York: Harcourt Brace

Barbalet, J. (1988) *Citizenship,* Milton Keynes: Open University Press

Bechofer, F. (1996) 'Comment on lockwood' *British Journal of Sociology* 47(3):551–5

Booth, W.J. (1994) 'On the idea of the moral economy' *American Political Science Review* 88(3):653–67

Bukodi, E., J. Goldthorpe, L. Waller and J. Kuha (2015) 'The mobility problem in Britain' *British Journal of Sociology* 66(1):93–117

Cameron, D. (2009) The age of austerity The Conservative Party | News | Speeches | David Cameron: The age of austerity (macropus.org) (accessed 23.2.24)

Cameron, D. (2010) Speech to the conservative party conference David Cameron's speech to the Tory conference: in full | Conservative conference 2010 | The Guardian 6 October (accessed 23.2.24)

Cameron, D. (2012) Prime Minister's message on welfare reform https://www.gov.uk /government/news/prime-ministers-message-on-welfare-reform (accessed 23.2.24)

Church Action on Poverty and Oxfam (2013) *Walking the Breadline,* Oxford: Oxfam

Clarke, J. and S. Newman (2012) 'The alchemy of austerity' *Critical Social Policy* 32(3):299–319

Clasen, J. and D. Clegg (2007) 'Levels and levers of conditionality: Measuring change within welfare states' in J. Clasen and N.A. Siegel (eds.) *Investigating Welfare State Change,* Cheltenham: Edward Elgar

Committee on Economic Social and Cultural Rights (1990) General comment No. 3: The nature of States parties' obligations (article 2, para. 1) (1990) | OHCHR (accessed 24.2.24)

CPAG (2014) *Written Case on Behalf of Child Poverty Action Group,* Intervention in SG and Ors v SSHD UKSC [2014] 0079

Douglas, M. (1986) *How Institutions Think,* Syracuse: Syracuse University Press

DWP (2010) *21st Century Welfare,* Cm7971, London: HMSO

Emirbayer, M. and A. Mische (1998) 'What is agency?' *American Journal of Sociology* 103(4):962–1023

End Hunger (2014) Open letter from Bishops – End hunger fast – End hunger fast 20 February (accessed 24.2.24)

Fassin, D. (2009) 'Moral economy revisited' *Annales. Histoire. Sciences Sociales* 64(6):1237–66

Financial Times (2023) Hunt to lay out budget plans to get sick and disabled back to work 12 March

Freeden, M. (1996) *Ideologies and Political Theory,* Oxford: Oxford University Press

Freeden, M. (2003) *Ideology: A Very Short Introduction,* Oxford: Oxford University Press

Gov.uk (2023) Government announces new welfare reforms to help thousands into work - GOV.UK (www.gov.uk) 5 September (accessed 24.2.24)

Guardian (2013) Benefit reforms will end 'something-for-nothing culture', says Duncan Smith | Iain Duncan Smith | The Guardian 1 October (access 23.2.24)

The Guardian (2014) Vulnerable man starved to death after benefits were cut | Benefits | The Guardian 28 February (accessed 24.2.24)

The Guardian (2016) DWP 'punishing' low-paid full-time workers under new benefits rule | Universal credit | The Guardian 14 April (accessed 23.2.24)

The Guardian (2020) Disabled man starved to death after DWP stopped his benefits | Disability | The Guardian 28 January (accessed 24.2.24)

The Guardian (2022) Soaring costs could strip 'basic dignity' from millions in UK | UK cost of living crisis | The Guardian 2 September (accessed 24.2.24)

The Guardian (2023) Unemployed who 'refuse to engage' could lose benefits in Hunt crackdown | Autumn statement 2023 | The Guardian 16 November (accessed 23.2.24)

The Guardian (2023a) People deemed unable to work 'face having benefits reduced under DWP plan' | Benefits | The Guardian 5 September (accessed 23.2.24)

The Guardian (2024) 'Seriously ill' mental health inpatients told to attend jobcentre or risk losing benefits | Welfare | The Guardian 10 February (accessed 23.2.24)

The Guardian (2024a) UK government's free childcare scheme in disarray, charities say | Childcare | The Guardian 15 January (accessed 23.2.24)

Harris, N. (2008) 'From unemployment to active jobseeking' in S. Stendahl, T. Erhag and S. Devetzi (eds.) *A European Work-First Welfare State*, Gothenburg: Centre for European Research, pp.49–77

HM Treasury (2015) *Summer Budget 2015*, London: HMSO, HC264

Kennedy, S. (2015) *Welfare Reform and Work Bill*, London: House of Commons Library, CBP 079252

Kennedy, S., C. Murphy and W. Wilson (2016) *Welfare Reform and Disabled People*, London: House of Commons Library, CBP 06294

Kennedy, S., A. Bate and R. Keen (2017) *The Two Child Limit in Tax Credits and Universal Credit*, London: House of Commons Library, CBP 7935

Laenen, T., F. Rossetti and W. Van Oorschot (2019) 'Why deservingness theory needs qualitative research' *International Journal of Comparative Sociology* 60(3):190–216

LBC (2023) Millions of unemployed Brits 'coasting on the hard work of taxpayers' to lose benefits 16 November (accessed 24.2.24)

Lockwood, D. (1996) 'Civic integration and class formation' *British Journal of Sociology* 47(3):531–50

Marshall, T.H. [1950] (1973) *Citizenship and Social Class*, in *Class, Citizenship and Social Development*, New York: Doubleday and Co., pp.65–122

Marshall, T.H. [1954] (1973) 'A note on status' in *Class, Citizenship and Social Development*, New York: Doubleday and Co., pp.200–8

Marx, K. [1943] (1975) 'On the Jewish question' in *Karl Marx and Frederick Engels: Collected Works*, Volume 3, New York: International Publishers, pp.146–74

Meuleman, B., F. Roosma and K. Abts (2020) 'Welfare deservingness opinion from heuristic to measurable concept' *Social Science Research* 85(January):102352

Millar, J. (2018) *Women, Work, and Welfare: Conditionality and Choice*. Institute for Policy Research, Bath: University of Both

Morris, L.D. (2020) 'Activating the welfare subject: The problem of agency' *Sociology* 54(2):275–91

Morris, L.D. (2021) *The Moral Economy of Welfare and Migration: Reconfiguring Rights in Austerity Britain*, London: McGill-Queens University Press

Munch, R. (2012) *Inclusion and Exclusion in the Liberal Competition State*, Abingdon: Routledge

Murphy, C. and R. Keen (2016) *Abolition of the Work Related Activity Component*, London: House of Commons Library, CBP 7649

Oakley, M. (2014) *Independent Review of the Operation of the Jobseekers Allowance Sanctions*, London: HMSO

Sayer, A. (2005) *The Moral Significance of Class*, Cambridge: Cambridge University Press

Sayer, A. (2007) 'Moral economy as critique' *New Political Economy* 12(2):261–70

Sayer, A. (2011) *Why Things Matter to People,* Cambridge: Cambridge University Press

Thompson, E.P. (1971) 'The moral economy of the English crowd in the eighteenth century' *Past and Present* 50(Feb):76–136

Van Oorschot, W. F. Roosma, B. Meuleman and T. Reeskens (eds.) (2017) *The Social Legitimacy of Targeted Welfare,* Cheltenham: Edward Elgar

Van Oorschot, W. (2008) 'Solidarity with immigrants in European welfare states' *International Journal of Social Welfare* 17(1):3–14

Weber, M.K.E. [1922] (1958) 'Class status and party' in H.H. Gerth and C.W. Mills (eds.) *From Max Weber: Essays in Sociology,* Oxford: Oxford University Press

Welfare Conditionality Project (2018) *Final Findings Report,* York: University of York

Wright, S. (2012) 'Welfare-to-work, agency and personal responsibility' *Journal of Social Policy* 41(2):309–28

Work and Pensions Committee (2019) *The Benefit Cap,* 24th Report of Session 2017–19, London: House of Commons, HC 1477

Work and Pensions Committee (2019a) *Universal Credit and "Survival Sex" – Work and Pensions Committee – House of Commons (parliament.uk)* 25 October (accessed 23.2.24)

Women's Budget Group (2017) *The Impact of Austerity on Black and Minority Ethnic Women in the UK,* London: Runnymede Trust

Legal Cases Cited

STEC and Ors v United Kingdom, GC 2005

Reilly and Wilson v SSWP [2013] UKSC 68

Hurley and Ors v SSWP [2015] EWHC 3382

SG and Ors v SSWP [2015] UKSC 16

CJ and SG v SSWP [2017] UKUT 0324

DA, DS and Ors v SSWP [2019] UKSC 21

3 Civic stratification and migrant rights

The previous chapter made reference to Hannah Arendt's [1948] (1979) understanding of citizenship and human rights, and notably her assertion that citizenship was the surest route for securing access to basic rights. Her writing on this topic provides a good entry point for thinking about the rights of non-citizens, or more specifically, trans-national migrants. Writing just before the launching of the UDHR, and in the absence of a developed system of international law, she was reflecting on the fact that outside of citizenship there was no effective means of claiming those rights that were notionally construed as 'inalienable' human rights. In fact, she deemed such rights to be an expression of 'hopeless idealism' (p.269), and argued that it was taken as read in the inter-war period that 'the law of a country could not be responsible for persons insisting on a different nationality' (p.275). Thus, in Arendt's terms 'the nation had conquered the state', which was a danger always inherent in the creation of the nation-state system.

We therefore arrive at Arendt's [1948] (1979:279) paradox – 'we became aware of the right to have rights…and a right to belong to some kind of organised community only when millions of people emerged who had lost and could not regain those rights'. The situation she describes refers to those people rendered stateless by the break-up of two multinational states of pre-war Europe (Russia and Austria-Hungary), who were perhaps most closely equivalent to the contemporary position of asylum seekers. But Arendt also notes that not all could be deemed political refugees, some having been expelled because of their race or class, while the living conditions of any alien, and even naturalised citizens, deteriorated with the presence of large numbers of the stateless. The outcome in each case was that the loss of national rights was identical to the loss of human rights, such that the plight of those affected was not the absence of a specific set of rights, but rather the loss of membership of a political community obligated to uphold such rights. So Arendt's paradox turns on the fact that the right to have rights rests on membership of a rights-granting community that has an obligation to honour the claim to a contingent set of rights. Thus, the loss of citizenship amounted to the absence of an effective means of access to 'inalienable' human rights, and any attempt to claim these

DOI: 10.4324/9781003324744-4

rights broke down when national states were confronted with the 'abstract nakedness of being human' (Arendt, [1948] 1979:299).

Despite the continuing resonance of Arendt's words, the timing of her argument is significant as a recognition of the challenge confronting the authors of the Universal Declaration of Human Rights (published in December 1948) and ensuing attempts to make it a reality. Since that time, however, a number of international instruments have been made available for ratification, and there now exists a formidable array of guarantees and protections beyond those attaching to citizenship, which many nation states undertake to uphold. In fact, for some, Arendt's paradox has now been reversed by the question of how the nation state as traditionally conceived can co-exist with the presence of significant numbers of non-nationals who hold an array of rights equivalent to citizenship. Hence, the announcement that 'a new and more universal concept of citizenship has unfolded in the 'post-national' era, one whose organising principles are based on universal personhood rather than national belonging' (Soysal, 1994:1).

Universal personhood

In direct contradiction with Arendt's argument, the assertion here is that 'incorporation into a system of membership rights does not inevitably require incorporation into the national collectivity' (Soysal, p.3). The change is attributed to the 'intertwining' of global and national discourses such that 'the global modalities of rights reverberate through nation-state-level arrangements and premises of citizenship' (p.6). Particular emphasis is placed on the argument that nation states are increasingly constrained by a global framework of human rights, which locates the source of legitimacy as related to rights within a trans-national order. Soysal (1994) clearly recognises that post-national developments have occurred while leaving intact the national regulation of immigration and a nation's control of its borders. However, these are presented in terms of 'discourses of the past' (p.8), in an argument that carries a sense of inevitability with respect to the collapse of nationally exclusive models of membership.

A more overtly normative orientation has also developed under the banner of 'cosmopolitanism', rooted in Kant's [1797] (2016) model for 'perpetual peace'. This model is based on a contract between nations that would mutually guarantee the security of national freedoms, while extending a cosmopolitan right of hospitality to strangers in peril. Contemporary elaborations of the cosmopolitan moment have developed along three dimensions (Beck and Sznaider, 2006) – a normative sensibility rooted in the universalist principles of human rights; a methodological sensibility that breaches the 'container' approach to society as a fixed and bounded national territory; and an empirical sensibility that documents concrete advances towards a more cosmopolitan world order. Scholarship on cosmopolitanism is perhaps less firm in its claims than the post-national argument, leaving more scope for an appreciation of the gap between ideal and reality, and hence Robert Fine's (2007:134) distinction between a 'cosmopolitan outlook' and the 'cosmopolitan condition'.

Both the post-national and cosmopolitan argument place due emphasis on the development of an established and enforceable framework of human rights, but both orientations also see scope for contradiction and complexity. Thus, for example, Soysal (1994:8) recognises a 'dialectical tension' between nationalist and universalist forces, while Fine (2007:140) in distinguishing between outlook and condition, observes that 'everything interesting occurs in the in-between'. However, the process whereby this 'in-between' is negotiated, and the nature of the malleable outcome(s) in terms of rights, has only gradually been subject to detailed attention. Hence the growing recognition that neither national closure nor post-national expansion offers an adequate basis for a full understanding of the migrant experience or the political responses it has provoked.

The terrain of rights engages a language of ethical certainty but manifests a practice of contestation and deliberation that often operates through legal procedure and is commonly advanced through civic activism, but only rarely yields 'self-evident' results. The mere existence of international instruments containing standards that are applicable to migrants (as listed by Soysal, 1994:184) is only a starting point for unpacking the force and the limits of trans-national guarantees. As noted in the previous chapter, even instruments overtly embracing universals make a distinction between absolute, limited and qualified rights, such that some rights can be subject to conditions related to national security or economic well-being, while even absolute rights raise difficult questions of interpretation. Rights can also be constrained in a variety of other ways, not least in requiring the signature and ratification of participating states for their implementation.[1] So, for example, the International Convention on the Protection of the Rights of All Migrant Workers and their Families has been ratified largely by sending countries, notably in North Africa and South America. No migrant-receiving state in Western Europe or North America has ratified the Convention, and nor have other significant destination countries.

Conventions can also be limited in other ways, and so may apply only to citizens of countries that are party to the convention, or only to those who are lawfully resident; many address the needs of specific groups, such as women, children, people living with disabilities, or relate to a specific area of rights. The establishment of the European Union, along with an EU citizenship, has commonly been cited as the most advanced instance of post-national society (Sassen, 1998; Soysal, 1994), with its own supra-national law and a dedicated

---

1 An exception would be customary international law, such as the prohibition on torture, which is assumed to have truly universal applicability.

court (the European Court of Justice) that supersedes domestic law. EU law confers the right to work and reside in any member state to all EU citizens (in fact to all citizens of European Economic Area (EEA) states),[2] but despite the importance placed on the free circulation of goods, services and people, this freedom of movement is limited to these citizens, and the full array of rights is only extended to those who move as 'workers'. Such internal freedoms have also been premised upon the intensification of control at the external borders of the union.

Civic stratification and migration

As should be apparent from even this brief sketch, an understanding of the rights available to non-citizens requires a clear grasp of the interplay between domestic, trans-national and supra-national law, their various modes of enforcement and the qualifying conditions of access that they variously contain. Thus, while the elaboration of a regime of rights that can be called upon to advance or secure the position of non-citizen migrants is beyond doubt, an emphasis on the growing power of 'universals' renders only incomplete understanding and can in fact be misleading. The outcome is rather a complex combination of rights and controls that affect different groups in different ways, to yield what Brubaker (1989:5) has termed the '*ad hoc* proliferation' of positions of partial membership – a development that has lacked an adequate theorisation. This is what Lockwood's (1996) concept of civic stratification potentially has to offer.

Lockwood himself was principally concerned with the inequalities generated within the status of citizenship, and in this sense he was most directly addressing Marshall's understanding of what had been deemed a unifying device. His only reference to the position of non-citizens is in relation to the case of '*gastarbeiter*' (Lockwood, 1996:541), which he sees as combining civic deficit with ethnic stigmatisation and partial civic exclusion, despite the payment of taxes. This interpretation makes an interesting contrast with Soysal's (1994) representation of German guest workers (two years prior to Lockwood's comment) as a group 'granted rights and protections by, and thus membership in, a state that is not "their own"'. We can only make sense of this apparent contradiction by fuller consideration of Brubaker's (1989) notion of partial membership, which can in turn benefit from an elaboration of the concept of civic stratification.

2 The terms of free movement under European law apply to all member states of the European Economic Area (EEA), and so extends to the additional countries of Iceland, Liechtenstein and Norway, and also Switzerland, which is a member of the single market.

Citizens and non-citizens, or members and non-members, each express a binary distinction, but as Brubaker's argument indicates, the position of trans-national migrants in their host community is more varied and complex than this allows. Hammar, writing in 1990, outlined a classic model in distinguishing between citizens, denizens and aliens. Denizen status refers to secure residence, and it is this status that is the basis for claims that citizenship has been superseded by residence. Permanent residence or 'settlement' carries the same array of rights as citizenship, with the notable exceptions of voting in national elections and freedom from deportation (though see below on the latter). However, outside of secure residence and citizenship, there is an extensive array of possible positions, and for a fuller account, we need to look more closely at the variety of possible legal statuses that a migrant might occupy. These statuses then dictate which rights may be granted or denied by the state, and hence amount to a form of civic stratification, with its varied positions determining 'who gets what'. They therefore constitute what, in the previous chapter, we termed the formal dimension of civic stratification, such that immigration status will dictate a migrant's inclusion or exclusion with respect to a range of basic rights. These statuses can be viewed as *category* distinctions, and as Clasen and Clegg (2007) have argued with respect to welfare rights, they may entail further elements of different treatment by virtue of both the particular *circumstances* of a claimant (e.g. income level), and the distinctive conditions of *conduct* that attach to a claim (e.g. to be law abiding).

Category distinctions in immigration law

Migrant categories are, of course, created by the system of immigration control and are not inherent features of the migrants themselves, but they distinguish between migrants with respect to their purpose of entry onto the national territory. Tourism aside, the possible bases for seeking entry are for work, family reasons, or protection, and in most cases a change of status after admission will be difficult or impossible to achieve, unless catered for by formalised rules of transition. The picture is of course made more complex in cases of EU membership, and in particular by the principle of free movement between member states, which will be considered separately below. Trans-national migration that does not fall under European law is governed by the visa regimes of potential host countries, which grant (or deny) entry and specify the accompanying terms and conditions. Other than free movement under EU law, admission for the purpose of employment lies in the gift of the state and will be governed by calculations based on the need for labour in terms of skills and occupation, and in relation to domestic supply.

Associated terms and conditions may specify a minimum income requirement, will possibly favour 'shortage occupations', and will also limit access to public funds – a term that covers the welfare system and the public health service – with full social rights only available once secure residence has been achieved, commonly after a minimum period of five years. In Britain, migrants who are 'subject to immigration control' (i.e. do not have secure residence) are required to pay a health surcharge,[3] regardless of the fact that they are already most probably paying tax, and are debarred from claiming welfare support. The transition to residence will usually require proof of self-maintenance and receipt of a minimum income, and this is one means of keeping a check on likely future demands for welfare support. In Britain the minimum income required for skilled workers has in recent years moved down from £35,800 to £25,600 (Guardian, 2020), but a rise to £38,700 was announced in December 2023 (Guardian, 2023). Workers who enter under schemes for temporary employment, or who earn below a designated minimum requirement are in most systems ineligible for transition to permanent residence (termed settlement). Thus, one example of distinctions of *circumstance* would be formally established rules governing differential treatment in relation to salary level.

Entry for family reasons also falls under a national visa regime, and usually occurs in cases of family unification, in relation to newly established partnerships, or family re-unification in relation to existing partnerships, children and possibly elderly parents. This mode of entry differs from entry for employment in that it is governed by national regulations, but must conform to international human rights commitments, notably the right to family life and the right to marry and found a family (articles 8 and 12 of the ECHR). In some countries (eg. Germany) family (re)unification is unconditional where the host member is a national citizen, and this is also the case in all EEA member states in relation to the (re)unification of families of EEA workers who have exercised freedom of movement (Morris, 2002). This has introduced a stratified element into family (re)unification requirements, in that a settled non-citizen non-EEA migrant will have to meet conditions based on proof of housing and maintenance, which in Britain also apply to British citizens seeking to bring a family member from overseas.

This constraint on UK citizens was deemed necessary because many migrants from Britain's ex-colonies held Citizenship of the UK and Colonies on arrival and control of family entry was therefore deemed necessary. However, there is a stratified element involved by virtue of the minimum income requirement for family (re)unification, which was raised quite substantially in 2012 and has proved prohibitive for many low-paid workers. A further planned rise from £18,600 to £38,700 was announced in December 2023 (Guardian, 2023). So the design of family (re)unification regulations provides an illustration of the distinction between category (which applies to

---

3 The health surcharge was introduced in 2015, with an exemption of health and care workers and their dependents announced in 2020 in response to the COVID pandemic and the need for key workers.

the type of migration) and circumstance, which applies to the ability to house and maintain.

A further differentiating element is the probationary period placed on incoming partners, which makes their presence in the country dependent on maintaining the marriage and debars them from claiming public funds until secure residence is achieved (after five years in Britain). It should also be noted that requirements for bringing elderly parents from abroad can be much more exacting than for partners, and have been heightened in Britain almost to the point of negating the right to family life in this context. Indeed, the purpose of the rules (Britcits v Secretary of State for the Home Department (SSHD) [2017] England and Wales Court of Appeal (EWCA) Civ 368, para 8) was to end the routine expectation of settlement for family members over 65 who are financially dependent on relatives in the UK, in view of the 'significant NHS and social care costs' this may entail.

A further form of migration that falls under international guarantees is asylum seeking, and here the purpose of entry is for protection. Asylum will be the focus of the following chapter, but for the moment, it should be noted that where nations have signed up to the Convention on the Status of Refugees, (commonly known as the Geneva Convention, 1951), they are committed to the principle of *non-refoulement* (not to return an asylum seeker to face a well founded fear of persecution), and must make some provision for their maintenance until a decision on their application has been made. The status of asylum seeker thus introduces a further rung to the civic stratification ladder, while the positive outcome of an application may result in full refugee status, or in some lesser form of protection. A refusal of asylum means that the applicant must leave the country, but in many cases will in practice feed the unknown number of undocumented migrants. The Home Office has recently revealed that it has no knowledge of the whereabout of 17,316 asylum seekers who withdrew their claim in the year ending September 2023 (Guardian, 2023b).

Undocumented migrants have no formal legal status (other than a negative one) and they occupy the lowest position within the system of civic stratification. In extending the notion of civic stratification to address the position of non-citizens, it is helpful to recognise that inclusion/exclusion will usually refer to access to a particular right or set of rights, and not to the total exclusion of a whole category. The position of undocumented migrants is the closest we come to the latter situation, though even the undocumented have basic rights such as equality before the law, or freedom from inhuman and degrading treatment. However, any attempt to claim such rights will require them to reveal their presence and status and would most probably lead to their deportation. An exception has sometimes been achieved by claims to inhuman and degrading treatment in relation to serious health care needs (Lowis, 2020).

EU law – another layer

This brief sketch of formal migrant statuses shows how the overall picture depends on the interplay between domestic law and national obligations under international law (encompassing human rights commitments and other international treaties) – but it is further complicated when EU law on free movement is engaged. Member states of the EU accordingly distinguish between migrants from other states that are members of the single market[4] and those whose entry has been governed by national immigration regulations, as constrained by human rights commitments under international law. EU law itself distinguishes between those citizens of EEA member states who arrive as 'workers' and qualify for equal treatment in social security, and those who enter in some other capacity (retirees, students, etc.) and who are obliged to maintain themselves. However, the distinctions do not stop there, and research has revealed many other differentiating factors, such that Amelina (2020) has addressed the entangled nexus of mobility and welfare that emerges from what she terms European cosmopolitanism and national welfare chauvinism.

As Amelina notes, the welfare magnet thesis has never been empirically proven, but she shows how in fact the interplay of different levels of regulations and requirements can be an obstacle for some types of movers, even under the purview of EU law. There is, for example, an assumption that movement is a one-time phenomenon, and hence regulations can hinder the acquisition of rights by those who are multiple movers or are simply endeavouring to live trans-national lives. Amelina thus suggests that it is possible to identify hierarchical boundaries of welfare that particularly disadvantage some groups, most notably the low-paid, low-skilled and precariously employed, and that the impacts can be different under different national regimes. Bruzelius (2019), for example, shows how administrative processes of residence registration shape conditionality rules and how the design of habitual residence requirements at the national level can have far-reaching effects, given this is itself a requirement for access to welfare. The forward-looking requirement of proof of intent to stay for at least one year (Sweden) presents difficulties for those on shorter employment contracts, while proof of residence may also be difficult where rules are backward-looking, such as to require evidence covering the previous three months (e.g. in Germany, three months past income from a German source). Both pose problems that are less likely to be encountered by citizen residents, and a requirement of proof of residence can also hinder the ability to qualify as a 'worker'.

4 Members of the EEA.

Other modes of civic stratification – gain and deficit

These then are some of the formal complexities that shape access to rights according to both category and circumstance, while conduct can apply with respect to behavioural requirements such as job search and reporting conditions internal to national welfare systems. Conduct can also apply in immigration decisions where issues of 'good character' come into play, as for example with transitions to secure residence or citizen status. But the actual experience of accessing rights – whether to work, to reside or to welfare – can also be affected by informal distinctions, most commonly yielding examples of civic deficit with regard to a formally held entitlement. So, where judgements about entitlement contain a discretionary or subjective element, the result could be a deficit – the failure to fully enjoy a right to which there is a formal entitlement.

Lockwood's original article identifies three types of deficit, as we saw in Chapter 1 – power deficit, stigmatised deficit and fiscal deficit, and we have also suggested the possible addition of discriminatory deficit, which could perhaps be viewed as a subdivision of stigmatised deficit. Of course, in the case of immigration, there is an inherent imbalance by virtue of the power of the national authority (the Home Office in the British case) to set out or oversee the terms – albeit under the constraints of international obligations or (where relevant) EU law. However, we can also find more specific instances: Lockwood's example of a power deficit is the unequal power held by employers when negotiating a contract – this then applies more strongly in the case of migration where, for example, only temporary or even undocumented work may be on offer. In extreme cases we can find forms of modern slavery and debt bondage (ATLEU, 2024). We can also detect a power deficit when it comes to defending a claim or challenging a decision, where the power balance can be swayed by the presence or absence of legal aid, or the ability to afford a private lawyer. We also saw in the discussion of freedom of movement under EU law that requirements for registering as resident and formal definitions of habitual residence can sometimes result in a deficit with respect to welfare entitlement.

However, perhaps the most obvious impact in relation to migration is stigmatised deficit where the negative perception attached to a particular status can itself amount to a deficit. This has been the case with the popular use of the label asylum seeker, or 'bogus' asylum seeker as a term of abuse, which detracts from the value of the status itself and erodes the moral standing of the individual in the eyes of the public. The designation 'illegal immigrant' has much the same effect, often erroneously applied to asylum seekers, who cannot by definition be illegal while their asylum claim is under consideration. Other examples can be found where the conditional requirements for a right are so harsh that in effect they prevent the exercise of the right, as can be the case with minimum salary requirements for family unification (as with the recent rise in British requirements noted above). We have also noted particularly stringent conditions for bringing elderly parents from overseas, such that in Britain the possibility has been all but abolished.

More overt deficits occur under what I have termed discriminatory deficit, so for example, what might be seen as a gender deficit arises when immigrant women from a failed (or even abusive) marriage are allowed to stay as the principal carer of their citizen child(ren) but (as in Britain) are debarred from public funds (and therefore welfare support). Although there is scope for this condition to be lifted, many women have difficulty furnishing the proof of destitution that this requires (Woolley, 2019). A shocking example of racially based deficit came to light in Britain as a result of the campaign to create 'a really hostile environment' for undocumented workers (Guardian, 2013b). In creating a criminal offence to work without permission, to employ someone without permission to work, or to rent property with cause to believe the tenant is unlawfully present (Yeo, 2017) the Home Office set off a chain response.

Landlords and employers took what were often discriminatory decisions over whether to rent a property or employ someone. Errors also extended to the NHS and the welfare system when people with a right of abode (usually offspring of the early 'Windrush' generation of immigrants), were unable to prove their status, having arrived as children and holding no documents. To compound their difficulties the Home Office had destroyed its own records, and as a result many lawfully resident or even citizen immigrants were variously denied health care, welfare support, employment and/or the right to remain, with tragic consequences. The individuals concerned suffered a deficit – or here we might even say an exclusion – through the denial of access to rights that were formally held. The Home Office management of this whole affair has been condemned by the Public Accounts Committee (2019) as complacent and neglectful.

Lockwood's third dimension of deficit is fiscal deficit, although he has little to say about this, beyond its being best understood negatively, as the converse of fiscal gain. However, when it comes to migration there are more direct examples that come to mind. The most obvious of these is the requirement for all workers to pay income tax but their exclusion from access to public funds (and therefore welfare rights) until they achieve settled status (usually after five years). Indeed, should a migrant worker have a significant spell of unemployment, not only could they be unable to claim welfare support, but they could be denied a transition to secure residence or even an extension of permission to remain. Migrants intending to stay for six months or more are required to pay an annual health surcharge in Britain, despite the fact that many are already paying income tax. Only when the role of migrants as key workers was highlighted by the COVID pandemic was an exemption made for health and care workers. Meyer and Bridgen (2022) provide a further example of fiscal deficit in Britain by showing how migrants with children (and prior to settlement) are made much more vulnerable to poverty by their lack of entitlement to child benefit or income related benefits. Given that such a family is almost certainly paying income tax and National Insurance, this is an example of fiscal deficit that has a particular impact on children. It is described by Meyer and Bridgen as the exclusion of new parents from the parental social contract, and the authors question its consistency with the Convention on the Rights of the Child.

In contrast with the impact of civic deficit, civic gain offers no particular instances that relate to migrant groups *per se*, and as Lockwood explains, it operates through the ways in which formally universal entitlements can confer unequal benefits. This may happen either in relation to power or prestige gains that operate through wealth and reputation, or fiscal gains that in practice 'work very substantially to the advantage of those who have income, wealth and know-how' (Lockwood, 1996:541–2), features that are much harder to accrue for most trans-national migrants, certainly within one generation. However, the remaining form of civic stratification – civic expansion, might be expected to hold very significant potential for the position of trans-national migrants, as in Lockwood's schema it flows from an inner logic by which citizenship and its related rights will always reach beyond their immediate constraints. It is perhaps faith in this dynamic that accounts for seemingly premature claims about the emergence of a 'post-national' society.

Civic expansion (and contraction)

We saw in Chapter 1 that civic expansion can occur for groups who are not in possession of the full array of rights – whether by virtue of formal exclusions or of significant deficits in their access and enjoyment. With respect to civic expansion, Lockwood (1996:543) notes that 'judicial review of legislation is a more and more frequent feature' of the push for a 'fuller citizenship'. However, for migrants, these efforts turn less on citizenship *per se*, but rather look towards universal human rights. Indeed, a key aspect of the post-national argument is that trans-national migrants have been increasingly able to draw upon claims based on 'universal personhood' to consolidate their position, in a drive for what could be termed civic expansion. Freeman (1995), though setting out from a focus on the national distinctiveness of immigration regimes, nevertheless detected an 'expansionary bias' that he viewed as common to the immigration policies of liberal democracies, sometimes in the face of popular opposition. The force of universalistic rights claims was central to his argument, as for example in relation to family (re)unification under the right to family life, though he did note a counter-tendency with regard to asylum.

Such an expansionary dynamic has commonly been seen – in Europe at least – as the means by which the migration that fed post-war reconstruction became permanent (see Soysal, 1994:33). However, the engagement of human rights claims in current struggles is more likely to be harnessed in attempts to arrest *contraction*, which we have noted is absent from

Lockwood's classification. Yet the civic stratification model still has much to offer for thinking about the dynamic nature of rights, and one route for further developing this potential is through a focus on the concept of 'moral resources', outlined in Chapter 1 and implicitly present in all discussions of the 'deserving' and 'undeserving'.

We saw from the discussion of the CARIN criteria in the previous chapter that in a ranking of deservingness based on control, attitude, reciprocity, identity and need, migrants tend to occupy the lowest position. Of course, public perceptions of each of these criteria are amenable to manipulation, but such perceptions are what shape the moral standing of migrants, and negative judgements will therefore erode the moral resources of their targets. This is the element of Lockwood's model that is most significant in driving the dynamic aspect of rights, and he makes reference to the link in his outline of expansion. However, as noted above, his framework neglects to consider contraction, and here the moral standing of a given group will often be the focus of active intervention by politicians and media outlets. A negative image of a particular group can lie behind a deficit in the delivery of rights, by (for example) clouding judgement with suspicion of fraudulent claims or other wrongdoing, as we saw in the Windrush scandal outlined above. Negative perceptions may also feature as justifications in the formal denial of rights, and we saw this in the run-up to Britain's referendum on membership of the European Union in 2016, when the social rights of EU migrants were formally limited in a variety of ways. Such denials are often preceded by negative campaigns intended to undermine perceptions of desert, and hence the moral standing of the target group.

This process of targeting has been analysed by Schneider and Ingram (1993) who argue that the social construction of target groups had been an overlooked phenomenon whereby the image of particular groups is harnessed by aspects of policy to enable or coerce behavioural change. The construction of target groups assists politicians' claims to be dealing with social problems and may be used to improve their election prospects. Although the authors do not single out migration as a paradigmatic example, it fits their analysis very well. According to Schneider and Ingram, there are four types of target – advantaged, contenders, dependents and deviants, and we can see some similarity to Lockwood's gain, expansion, deficit and exclusion. 'Advantaged' groups are the recipients of positive policy benefits, 'contenders' have the moral power to improve their treatment, 'dependents' are passive and powerless, and 'deviants' are the subjects of punishment and coercion. Schneider and Ingram also speak of pendulum swings in policy such that groups can move from one position to another, and here efforts to influence public perceptions can be a crucial issue.

Moral resources and moral economy – the Brexit case

The previous chapter made reference to a key argument advanced by Munch's (2012) discussion of inclusion and exclusion in policy design, namely that political rhetoric can shape the way problems – or problem groups – are perceived and tackled. This is especially the case in relation to migration, which is a key site of political intervention, insofar as public sentiment towards migrants is somewhat volatile and ripe for manipulation. So the idea of a 'moral economy' – or more particularly the process of its construction – can again be brought to bear in relation to the position of trans-national migrants and their access to 'moral resources', or what we can call their moral standing in society. The recent history of British immigration policy provides a striking example of this process in operation, especially in the run-up to the referendum on membership of the European Union.

Early signs of a 'moral panic' related to free movement between the member states of Europe can be found in fall-out from the lifting of labour restrictions on the entry of Bulgarians and Romanians under EU law, as of January 2014. In preparation for the change, and in the context of inflated estimates of the number of arrivals to be expected (Guardian, 2013), the UK government rushed through changes to restrict access to benefits and public services. The Council of Europe's Human Rights Commissioner spoke against the accompanying 'shameful rhetoric' that targeted Romanian and Bulgarian migrants and 'risked feeding stereotypes and hostility', to argue that:

> A stigma is put on Bulgarian and Romanian citizens just because of their origin. This is unacceptable because a state cannot treat Bulgarian and Romanian citizens differently from other EU citizens. They need to be treated as everyone else, not on the basis of assumptions or generalisations about their ethnic origin.
>
> (Guardian, 2013a)

He called on British political leaders to take a more positive role in defusing heated debate about immigration, and to make clear the positive contribution made by migrant workers, but policy and discourse in Britain took the opposite path.

In launching the referendum of 2016 David Cameron (the then Prime Minister) had hoped to consolidate support for continuing membership of the EU, albeit with some reform of the terms of free movement, but his case for reform instead contributed to support for withdrawal. As with the welfare reforms, an associated rhetoric hinged on fairness to the 'hard-working taxpayer' (Cameron, 2013), but with the crucial addition that breaking the 'cycle of dependency' in relation to welfare meant 'sorting out welfare and migration', which were to be addressed as 'two sides of the same coin' (Cameron, 2011). In effect, this argument set British welfare claimants against EU migrants, who under the terms of free movement had a right to equal treatment in relation to social security. Claims of the need to end the 'something for nothing culture' among migrants (Cameron, 2013) and to address 'rogue

EU benefit claims' (DWP, 2013) amounted to an attack on the moral standing of EU migrants, which set the scene for an erosion of their rights.

As with the welfare reform (see Chapter 2), we again see an example of Freeden's (1996, 2003) argument on the translation of abstract concepts into concrete content, which can also set up an opposition between particular social groups or behaviour patterns. We can make a link here with Laclau's approach to the analysis of political discourse, which points to the way that key aspects of a discourse can be viewed in terms of mutual affinities or oppositions in what he terms the logic of equivalence and difference (Laclau, 2014:68). These groupings can then be analysed in terms of the construction of equivalential chains – chains made up of linked concepts and behaviours, and which demonstrate the way a discourse has the potential to unite or divide social groups according to their standing in relation to the issues in play. We can apply this insight to the discursive opposition that sets fairness for the hard-working taxpayer against dependency and abuse from welfare claimants, while also setting welfare claimants or 'the British people' against EU migrants.

The measures that followed placed a time limit on the duration of welfare support for unemployed EEA migrants, and also removed their access to child benefit, housing benefit, and child tax credits (see Kennedy, 2015 for details), while in March 2015 regulations were passed by Parliament to exclude EEA jobseekers from Universal Credit. In fact, official sources show EEA nationals did not disproportionately claim benefits (Keen and Turner, 2016), while the Social Security Advisory Committee and the Migration Advisory Committee (MAC) (among others) have noted the absence of evidence showing benefits as a reason for migration (MAC, 2014; Kennedy, 2015b:26). Furthermore, the effect of migrant presence on jobs and wages at that time was calculated to be extremely slight (Devlin et al., 2014). Nevertheless, the rhetorical battle is what appears to have shaped public perceptions and in terms of civic stratification we have seen an attack on the moral standing of EEA migrants, and an attendant erosion of both their moral and material resources, both of which served as a prelude to the reduction of their rights. The misguided nature of this approach by the then Prime Minister is now a matter of history, and his rhetoric was one of the factors that tipped the referendum result against 'Remain', precipitating his resignation.

Hence, the run-up to the referendum and Cameron's attempt to modify the rights associated with free movement provide one instance of the way political rhetoric seeks to shape public perceptions and the moral standing of a given group in society. The rhetoric surrounding EU workers overshot its aim in so far as it seems to have encouraged support for Leave, by the classic construction of EEA migrants as 'undeserving'. Ironically, support for migration has now increased with labour shortages in the fallout from Brexit and greater public awareness of the role of migrants as key workers in the pandemic (ONS.gov.uk, 2020). But the attack on free movement was only one dimension of a wider attempt to reduce net migration to an unrealistic target of 'tens of thousands' per year (Guardian, 2020a), and here we see a moral economy at work in the fuller elaboration of conditionality as pertaining to migrants rights. This again revolved around a particular conception of 'fairness' and now, in post-Brexit Britain, it affects all trans-national migration.

Conditionality and contestation

So far, in the case of Britain, we have noted a continuity between welfare policy and immigration policy (see Morris, 2021 for a full account), which despite setting welfare claimants and migrants in opposition adopt the same devices of control to both – notably applying conditionality shaped by conceptions of desert, and engaging differences of category, circumstance and conduct. Heightened conditionality has been used in Britain alongside withdrawal from EU membership to pursue an unrealistic aim in the reduction of net immigration, and as with other regimes the conditions imposed for access to national territory and rights are in practice markers of desert. However, Chauvin and Garces-Mascarenas (2012) argue that even undocumented migrants may avail themselves of what they term 'circuits of incorporation' (p.241) which often turn on furnishing proof of presence, good conduct and fiscal contribution – the 'emblems of good citizenship' (p.243). Similarly, Landolt and Goldring (2015) approach conditionality for non-citizens as a multi-scalar 'assemblage' constructed by actors within a system of power, regulation and bureaucratised administration but embedded in a moral framework of desert. Both sets of writers wish to emphasise the possibilities of incorporation even within a restrictive system, and both note that tensions and contradictions often arise within the law, or from a fraught combination of policy, law and practice.

These arguments can readily be accommodated by the concept of civic stratification, which is then enriched by the addition. The conditions that govern the entry of migrants and the designation of the varied immigration statuses also cover what Hammar (1990) terms rules of transition, so a system of stratified rights contains within it the possibility of movement upwards or downwards. It is even possible (albeit extremely lengthy and demanding) to move through several stages from undocumented status to security of stay, or indeed to make the reverse journey. Such transitions may be foreseen and planned by the system, or may occur when different aspects of law and practice come into conflict. We saw above that modes of conditionality for workers can rest on meeting requisite skill and salary levels, minimum income requirements for family (re)unification, exclusion from accessing public funds until securing permanent residence (settlement), meeting specified 'exceptional circumstances' for lifting such an exclusion, or for a transition from undocumented status. We noted in Britain a tightening of all these conditions, which was also accompanied by the attempt to create a 'hostile environment' designed to make survival for undocumented migrants prohibitively difficult. The overall effect can be summarised as follows:

> a stratified system of control that places limits and conditions on entry, erodes entitlement for those present, makes challenge more difficult the more marginal one's position, impugns the moral standing of migrants by assumptions of resource drain/or abuse, and reduces the scope for compassion within the system.
>
> (Morris, 2021:124)

Where such regulations and requirements are driven by an overtly hostile rhetoric, as was the case in 'austerity' Britain, the question arises of whether and how they can be contested, especially since the drive for reduction of net migration both reflected and reinforced public concerns – 77% of the population at the time believed that immigration was too high (Independent, 2014). In Lockwood's formulation civic expansion (but even moreso contesting contraction) depends on bringing moral or material resources to bear in arguments for an improved position with respect to rights. Given that such resources do not usually fall within the scope of individual action, then the expansion (or restoration) of rights will rest on the intervention of 'civic activists' – often located within, or working in collaboration with voluntary sector organisations. Such organisations intervene both by bringing their own moral and material resources to bear through public campaigning, and by seeking out test cases through which to challenge contentious policy measures and thus advance the position of their client group(s). According to Lockwood (1996:543), 'civic activism proper is the vocation of a small minority' but he adds that its power is not to be underestimated.

Contesting contraction

As we saw in relation to welfare policy, legal challenge is one important mode of contestation, especially in the face of official discourse that fosters public hostility to migration. Such challenges operate through judicial review of test cases, and mean that the courts can serve as a public arena for the airing of arguments against a particular policy measure (cf Habermas, 1996), and though the principle of parliamentary sovereignty is strong it is not absolute. We find arguments against the rationality of policy, albeit measured against the legitimacy of government objectives, and also challenges to their legality, with respect both to domestic law and conformity with international treaty obligations, most notably human rights commitments. The presentation of evidence, and even judicial rulings, can also stray over into a more overtly moral terrain that goes beyond the narrow remit of the law, though deliberation will ultimately turn on the legal purchase of claims from those whose 'deservingness' has been impugned. Nevertheless, a successful case could conceivably restore the 'moral standing' of the claimants, and in the case of trans-national migrants will also serve to test out arguments about post-national expansion, in the specific context of individual rights claims.

A number of examples can be furnished from recent challenges in British courts during the austerity period in which the (then) government embraced its unachievable aim of reducing net migration to tens of thousands – an aim recently repeated (Guardian 25.11.22) despite a net migration record of 745,000 for the year to December 2022 (Guardian, 2023c). One example comes from a challenge to the implementation of a statutory limit of three months on welfare support for *jobless* EEA migrants (as detailed above). *Established* EEA workers who became unemployed were limited to six months JSA, and thereafter lost worker status, and this in turn rebounded on their path to permanent residence. At the same time, a minimum earnings threshold was introduced to guide assessments of worker status – i.e. whether an EEA migrant qualified for rights *as a worker* – affecting potential access to other benefits. As O'Brien (2015) notes, this was especially likely to penalise single parents.

We have already pointed to evidence that undermines the rationale for Cameron's 'two sides of the same coin' approach. Nevertheless, British conditionality went beyond what was acceptable under EU case law, (Case C-292/89 [1997] ECR I-00745) whereby eligibility for benefit requires evidence of continuing job search and a genuine chance of being engaged. This stood in contrast to much stronger DWP guidance, which required 'compelling evidence of a genuine prospect' of work, and the anti-poverty NGO, CPAG (Williams, 2015), compiled and published a range of arguments that could be made against the lawfulness of this test. When a legal challenge was brought against DWP practice, the Upper Tribunal (Case C-292/89 [1997] ECR I-00745) cautioned against raising the bar beyond the level required under EU law of a 'real prospect' within a 'reasonable period'. So here was a challenge that succeeded at the margins, and though it did not amount to a full assault on the whittling away of jobseeker rights, it did serve as a warning against an overly restrictive approach by the then government. It has now, of course, been superseded by Britain's withdrawal from the EU.

A different example – one that directly engages human rights obligations – was the challenge to an increased minimum income requirement for family (re)unification to a level of £18,600 *per annum* for a spouse, with additions for children – effective from July 2012 (Gower, 2014). This is significantly more demanding than the previous regime and is now in fact scheduled to increase even further.[5] The sum of £18,600 was chosen as the amount at which a family would not be eligible for income-related benefits and was defended by the argument that incoming migrants must be able to integrate and that 'family

5 To rise in phases to £38,700 by 2023 (Guardian, 2023a).

life must not be established in the UK at the taxpayer's expense' (Gower, 2014:17). At the time that this change was made, the probationary period during which an incoming partner is denied access to public funds was also increased from two to five years. Criticism of the raised minimum income requirement, furnished by the migrant advisory NGO Joint Council for the Welfare of Immigrants (JCWI), pointed to the exclusion from the calculation of additional income sources, such as well-evidenced third-party support or the prospective earnings of an incoming partner. It was also argued that the rules in practice could increase the need for welfare support by restricting the working hours of a sponsor parent due to childcare responsibilities that an incoming partner could relieve.

A legal challenge on the basis of discrimination by virtue of the impact on low-paid groups and hence on ethnic minorities and women (a stratifying effect in terms of access to the right) was dismissed as proportionate to the legitimate aims of the policy (MM v SSHD [2014] EWCA Civ 985, para 155). However, the Convention on the Rights of the Child and S55 of 2009 Borders Citizenship and Immigration Act require government policy to safeguard and promote the welfare of children in discharging its immigration functions. A judgment from the Supreme Court (MM and Ors [2017] UKSC 10, para 92) therefore found the rules to be unlawful in failing to give effect to these duties, though the result was somewhat limited. In response, the government allowed for the adjustment of requirements in exceptional circumstances, but the ruling again delivers a cautionary message to the government.

A further example took recourse to the absolute right of protection from inhuman and degrading treatment – as interpreted in the Limbuela case (see Morris, 2010) – in response to the denial of access to public funds for parents granted leave to remain on human rights grounds. The ban may be lifted where exceptional circumstances pertain, and a pressing case was made in research conducted with the practical and financial support of voluntary sector actors (see Woolley, 2019). As a result of the ensuing legal challenge, official guidance on when this exception may be applied, or when the condition should not imposed, was ruled unlawful (*R (and litigation friend J) v SSHD* [2020] EWHC 1299 (Admin)). A key determining factor was whether the claimant must already be suffering destitution, or whether it was sufficient to show that this condition was imminent. The judge found the guidance to be inadequate in failing to identify the legal duty to provide support in order to *avoid* inhuman and degrading treatment (para 71) – so imminent destitution was sufficient.

These few examples illustrate the fact that the granting or denial of rights is part of a dynamic process in which legal challenge can be initiated or supported by virtue of the moral and material resources proffered by civic activists in the course of exposing government policy to scrutiny. The result may only amount to small changes at the margins, but may still serve to bolster the 'moral standing' of a particular claimant group – though a more negative backlash could also be possible. While Lockwood's framework sees moral and material resources to be active ingredients in the expansion of rights, we find above that they are also called into play by the engagement of civic activists in challenges to arrest or to limit contraction.

The fragility of citizenship rights

There remains one further issue of note, and that is the possibility of an erosion of the rights of citizens. We began this chapter with a reference to Arendt's [1948] (1979) argument that without membership of a rights-granting community through citizenship, there was no meaningful access to 'the right to have rights'. Freedom from deportation has been one of the few remaining privileges of citizenship, but this picture is now changing. For example, the Nationality and Borders Act of 2022 permitted the removal of British citizenship in cases of a threat to national security and where the individual concerned had access to an alternative citizenship. The provision is interesting with respect to civic stratification, in that it creates two categories of citizen, one of whom cannot be deprived of their citizenship, and the other – most likely a second or third generation migrant, and most probably from an ethnic minority – for whom citizenship is not an absolute guarantee.

One recent case has been the removal of British citizenship from Shamima Begum, who left Britain in 2015 as a 15 year old school girl to join the Islamic State in Syria. Once there, she was married to an IS fighter and gave birth to three children, all of whom died. When she was discovered in 2019, the then Home Secretary Sajid Javid revoked her British citizenship in a decision that has been upheld by the Supreme Court (Begum v SSHD [2021] UKSC 7). She appealed without success to the Special Immigration Appeals Commission (SIAC appeal no. SC/163/2019 22 February 2023) under the argument that she had in effect been exiled for life when there should have been an investigation into whether she was a child victim of trafficking, recruited and transported for the purpose of sexual exploitation. Her appeal against this decision has also failed, though the case raises questions of her right to protection under provisions for victims of trafficking, and as a minor, as against the national security concerns of the state, However, the court has taken the view that the decision was procedurally fair and the dismissal of her appeal effectively renders her stateless and seemingly bereft of 'the right to have rights'. This is more powerfully the case, given that Shamima Begum's alternative (Bangladeshi) citizenship only applied until she was 21 years old; she is now 24. As Tripkovic (2021:1056) has argued, this is not a case of corrective punishment, which is in principle at least, an inclusionary project, but is rather a step of eradication by virtue of the removal of 'expendable' citizens from the polity. In fact, the Illegal Migration Act of 2023 now permits revocation of citizenship without prior notice, hence inhibiting appeals. Here again we have a case in which the differential granting (or denial) of rights is fraught with questions that revolve around both national interests and universal protections, in a manner barely separable from notions of desert and moral standing.

References

Amelina, A. (2020) 'European welfare between complex regulatory frameworks and mobile Eureopean's experiences of social (in)security' in A. Amelina, E. Carmel, A. Runfors and E. Scheibelhofer (eds.) *Boundaries of European Citizenship*, pp.1–18

Anti-Trafficking and Labour Exploitation Unit (ATLEU) (2024) Challenge to government's Seasonal Worker Scheme — ATLEU 26 January (accessed 24.2.24)

Arendt, H. [1948] (1979) *The Origins of Totalitarianism*, New York: Harcourt Brace

Beck, U. and N. Sznaider (2006) 'Unpacking cosmopolitanism for the social sciences' *British Journal of Sociology* 57(1):1–23

Brubaker, W.R. (1989) *Immigration and the Politics of Citizenship in Europe and America*, Lanham MD: University Press of America

Bruzelius, C. (2019) 'Freedom of movement, social rights and residence based conditionality in the European Union' *Journal of European Social Policy* 29(1):70–83

Cameron, D. (2011) David Cameron on immigration: Full text of the speech | David Cameron | The Guardian 14 April (accessed 27.2.24)

Cameron, D. (2013) https://www.gov.uk/government/speeches/david-camerons-immigration-speech 25 March (accessed 27.2.24)

Chauvin, S. and B. Garces-Mascarenas (2012) 'Beyond informal citizenship' *International Political Sociology* 6(3):241–59

Clasen, J. and D. Clegg (2007) 'Levels and levers of conditionality: Measuring change within welfare states' in J. Clasen and N.A. Siegel (eds.) Investigating Welfare State Change, Cheltenham: Edward Elgar, pp.166–97

Department of Work and Pensions (2013) https://www.gov.uk/government/news/accelerating-action-to-stop-rogue-eu-benefit-claims 18 December (accessed 27.2.24)

Devlin, C., O. Bolt, D. Patel, D. Harding and I. Hussain (2014) *Impact of Migration on UK Native Employment*, Occasional Paper No. 109, London: Home Office/ Department for Business and Innovation Skills

Fine, R. (2007) *Cosmopolitanism*, Abingdon: Routledge

Freeden, M. (1996) *Ideologies and Political Theory*, Oxford: Oxford University Press

Freeden, M. (2003) *Ideology: A Very Short Introduction*, Oxford: Oxford University Press

Freeman, G.P. (1995) 'Modes of immigration politics in liberal democratic states' *International Migration Review* 29(4):881–902

Gower, M. (2014) *The Financial Requirement for Spousal Visas*, London: House of Commons Library, SN/HA/06724

The Guardian (2013) Romanian and Bulgarian migration estimates are 'unfounded', says report | Immigration and asylum | The Guardian 18 August (accessed 27.2.24)

The Guardian (2013a) European watchdog accuses Britain of shameful rhetoric on migrants | Immigration and asylum | The Guardian 29 March (accessed 27.2.24)

The Guardian (2013b) Immigration bill: Theresa May defends plans to create 'hostile environment' | Theresa May | The Guardian 10 October (accessed 27.2.24)

The Guardian (2020) Government reduces minimum salary for migrants to settle in UK | Migration | The Guardian 24 October (accessed 26.2.24)

The Guardian (2020a) 10 years on, David Cameron's toxic net migration pledge still haunts the UK | Daniel Trilling | The Guardian 14 January (accessed 27.2.24)

The Guardian (2023) Five-point plan to cut UK immigration raises fears of more NHS staff shortages | Immigration and asylum | The Guardian 4 December (accessed (26.2.24)

The Guardian (2023a) Tell us: Will you be affected by the UK visa rule changes? | Migration | The Guardian 5 December (accessed 26.2.24)

The Guardian (2023b) Home office 'loses' 17,000 people whose asylum claims were withdrawn | Immigration and asylum | The Guardian 29 November (accessed 26.2.24)

The Guardian (2023c) Net migration to UK hit record 745,000 in 2022, revised figures show | Immigration and asylum | The Guardian 23 November (accessed 27.2.24)

Habermas, J. (1996) *Between Facts and Norms,* Cambridge: Polity Press

Hammar, T. (1990) *Democracy and the Nation State,* Aldershot: Avebury

The Independent (2014) Anti-immigrant feeling in Britain is on the rise as more than half want cut in numbers, according to major new research | The Independent | The Independent 7 January (accessed 13.3.24)

Kant, I. [1797] (2016) *Perpetual Peace,* Amazon GB

Keen, R. and R. Turner (2016) *Statistics on Migrants and Benefits,* London: House of Commons Library, BP 7445

Kennedy, S. (2015) *Measures to Limit Migrants' Access to Benefits,* London: House of Commons Library, BP 06889

Laclau, E. (2014) *The Rhetorical Foundations of Society,* London: Verso

Landolt, P. and L. Goldring (2015) 'Assembling non-citizenship through the work of conditionality' *Citizenship Studies* 19(8):853–69

Lockwood, D. (1996) 'Civic integration and class formation' *British Journal of Sociology* 47(3):531–50

Lowis, J. (2020) https://ohrh.law.ox.ac.uk/uk-supreme-court-relaxes-the-test-for-establishing-a-breach-of-article-3-in-medical-removal-cases/ 3 May (accessed 10.3.24)

MAC (2014) *Migrants in Low-skilled Work,* London: Home Office

Meyer, T. and P. Bridgen (2022) 'Open for the childless skilled only' *Journal of Poverty and Social Justice* 30(1):9–36

Morris, L.D. (2002) *Managing Migration: Civic Stratification and Migrants Rights,* Abingdon: Routledge

Morris, L.D. (2010) *Asylum, Welfare and the Cosmopolitan Ideal,* London: Glasshouse Press

Morris, L.D. (2021) *The Moral Economy of Welfare and Migration: Reconfiguring Rights in Austerity Britain,* London: McGill-Queens University Press

Munch, R. (2012) *Inclusion and Exclusion in the Liberal Competition State,* Abingdon: Routledge

O'Brien, C. (2015) 'The pillory, the precipice, and the slippery slope' *Journal of Social Welfare and Family Law* 37(1):111–36

ONS.gov.uk (2020) Coronavirus and non-UK key workers – Office for National Statistics (ons.gov.uk) 8 October (accessed 27.2.24)

Sassen, S. (1998) *Globalisation and its Discontents,* New York: The New Press

Schnieder, A. and H. Ingram (1993) 'The social construction of target populations' *American Political Science Review* 87(2):334–47

Soysal, Y. (1994) *Limits of Citizenship,* Chicago: University of Chicago Press

Tripkovic, M. (2021) 'Transcending the boundaries of punishment' *British Journal of Criminology* 61(4):1044–65

Williams, M. (2015) *Kapow to the GPOW,* London: GPAG

Woolley, A. (2019) Access denied access denied: The cost of the 'no recourse to public funds' policy | St Martin in the Field (frontlinenetwork.org.uk) 17 June (accessed 24.2.24)

Yeo, C. (2017) Everything you need to know about the hostile environment for immigrants https://www.freemovement.org.uk/hostile-environment-affect/ 17 May (accessed 12.3.24)

Legal Cases Cited

Case C-292/89 [1997] ECR I-00745

Britcits v SSHD [2017] EWCA Civ 368

R (and litigation friend J) v SSHD [2020] EWHC 1299 (Admin)

4 Asylum and civic stratification

At first glance, requests for asylum and the granting of refugee status seem to imply a much simpler configuration than the complexities of immigration status described in the previous chapter, but the recent history of asylum may be characterised by varied and shifting categories of legal status and their associated rights. The very concept of the refugee, as derived from the interpretation and application of the Convention on the Status of Refugees (CSR, also know as the Geneva Convention, 1951), and other (lesser) forms of protection that may flow from human rights guarantees, each rest on a process of classification. In addition to the distinctions involved, we have seen an increase in both the extent and variety of the underlying phenomena associated with forced migration, which can stem not only from oppressive regimes but also from war, intra-state conflict, natural disaster, climate change, etc. As a minimum, at any given time, there will be those who wish to make a claim for asylum (asylum seekers), those who have been recognised as (CSR) refugees, those owed some form of subsidiary protection, and others who are deemed not to qualify. Even among the unsuccessful, there are distinctions to be made such as whether there are genuine obstacles to removal, and whether minor-age children are involved. These distinctions are just the beginning for an understanding of the complex and shifting dynamics that underpin what Zetter (2007:173) has termed a labelling process, whereby 'bureaucratic interests and procedures...are themselves crucial determinants in the definition of labels like refugee...not only to describe the world but also to construct it in convenient images'. It is recognition of such a process that underpins his account of a 'fractioning' of the status of a refugee, and the accompanying proliferation of labels whose associated institutional practices have relentlessly curtailed the rights and assistance afforded.

Quite how far sovereign power and techniques of governance that seek to limit entry and stay on national territory can be maintained or superseded remains a perplexing question. In Hannah Arendt's [1948] (1979) classic formulation of the right to have rights, her reflections on the stateless populations that emerged from the inter-war period in Europe came to rest on 'the constitutional inability of European nation-states to guarantee human rights to those

DOI: 10.4324/9781003324744-5

who had lost nationally guaranteed rights'. Hence, her conclusion that 'no such thing as inalienable human rights existed' (Arendt, [1948] 1979:269). Since her time of writing, however, we have seen the CSR guarantee of non-refoulement – the prohibition on returning someone to face probable persecution – acquire a status close to customary international law. Indeed, it was possible for Zetter (2007:180) to write, albeit with a backward gaze, that 'refugee status has remained the only systematic and relatively accessible route for large-scale, globalized migration'.

Yet Johnson [2014] (2018) has more recently documented what she terms a paradigm shift; a movement away from the basic distinction between voluntary and forced migration, and towards a more restrictive distinction between regular and irregular entry, whereby the focus of control is turned upon what was previously a protected category. It is the spontaneous refugee who is now perceived as the greatest threat to the ultimate sovereign power – control over entry and stay – and the paradigm shift Johnson speaks of is driven by a desire on the part of states to establish fuller control over access to 'protection'. Hence, the simple binary distinction of regular/irregular (Johnson, [2014] 2018), or in Squire's terms the desirable and undesirable, has been viewed as the expression of an attempt to reassert a territorial order that maps more directly onto a national political community (Squire, 2009). However, Squire argues that the nation state can offer only an inherently unstable basis for a territorial social order, and that these simple oppositions scarcely hint at the ensuing complexity. Confronted by both the 'turbulence of migration' and forms of oversight and protection that might seem to challenge national authority, the outcome is rather 'a complex play of inclusionary and exclusionary forces' (Squire, 2009:35; see also Morris, 1997), that together produce the fragmentary patterns identified by Zetter. The underlying process is captured by what Landolt and Goldring (2015) more broadly term the 'assemblage' of non-citizen status, as noted in the previous chapter; a dynamic multi-scalar process, built up through the incremental interplay of social actors, power relations, discursive frames, regulatory systems and bureaucratic administration. It is here that the notion of civic stratification might be brought to bear, and in fact, it can operate with respect to several dimensions of the refugee/asylum-seeking experience. The starting point is access to the status determination process itself, followed by its possible outcomes in terms of formal status. We can then consider the treatment of pending, successful and unsuccessful claimants in relation to maintenance and survival, and finally the political discourse that lies behind the shifting contours of this whole phenomenon. All turn on stratified access to rights and protections.

Access to status determination

The CSR definition of a refugee is someone who

owing to a well founded fear of being persecuted for reasons of race, religion, nationality, membership of a particular social group, or political opinion is outside the country of *his* nationality and is unable, or owing to such fear, is unwilling to avail *himself* of the protection of that country.

(United Nations (UN), 1951)

It offers an interesting echo of Kant's [1797] (2016:40) foundational cosmopolitan right, expressed in his essay Perpetual Peace as a right to hospitality for those who cannot be turned away without risk of their destruction. However, while several instruments of international law embrace a right to seek asylum, there is no water-tight obligation to grant it, and so Jack Straw (2000), speaking as British Home Secretary, was able to assert: 'The Convention gives us the obligation to consider any claims made within our territory...but no obligation to facilitate the arrival on our territory of those who wish to make a claim'. Alongside an ostensible acceptance of the principle of protection, states have exploited this anomaly to the maximum by a number of devices that seek to establish control at a distance. These include the imposition of visa requirements on refugee-producing countries, the use of carrier sanctions that impose fines on companies transporting passengers with inadequate documentation, liaison officers situated at points of departure, and increasingly detection by radar or drone of vessels seeking entry to national waters. In other words, we see a cumulative extension of migration control beyond the physical borders of the state (Gammeltoft-Hansen, 2011), to which we can add the creation of 'buffer zones' in critical locations[1] and the growing incidence of 'pushbacks' both by sea and by land. And note that repulsion into a desert region can be just as perilous in this context as the abandonment of struggling vessels at sea. In practice, these forms of governing at a distance have had a stratifying effect on the opportunity to lodge a claim for protection.

The most recent and perhaps the most extreme of such devices involves interception at sea, with a related continuum of outcomes, running from status determination in the hoped for destination, through delivery to a third country willing to undertake this processing, pushback with no clear destination, return to the point of departure, or effective abandonment at sea, at worst resulting in death (see Guardian, 2022a). When narrowly framed as marine interdiction the exercise is explicitly designed to repel intercepted vessels, together with their human cargo, but when this cargo is wholly or in part made up of passengers seeking asylum then the question of access to status determination inevitably arises. Hence, maritime interdiction sits in close proximity to the growing practice of 'offshoring' the whole asylum process.

---

1 E.g. the eastern borders of the EU before the accession of the border states.

According to the UN Convention on the Law at Sea (UNCLOS, 1994) National territory extends 12 nautical miles from the coast and therefore falls under the sovereignty of state power to eject vessels carrying passengers in violation of immigration law. Such actions must, however, comply with other aspects of international law – most notably for our purposes here the principle of non-refoulement. A contiguous zone that extends for 24 nautical miles from the coast confers a more limited right to police, but the area remains subject to international law, including refugee law (Moreno-Lax, 2021). There is also a universal obligation to render assistance to those in distress at sea, though this obligation runs up against the (often prioritised) interests of immigration control, as reflected in some cases by a reluctance to accept disembarkation on the territory of the rescuing authority. Rescue may well function as a disguise for interdiction and control, though push-back with little or no pretence of rescue seems to be a growing practice.

US interception and return of asylum seekers has targeted various incoming groups over time, but the paradigm case – and an early form of this elision – began in the 1980s with the attempted arrival by sea of large numbers of Haitians (see Ghezelbash, 2018; Moreno-Lax, 2021). Initially held on coastguard cutters outside of territorial waters, they were assessed by summary screening for 'credible fear', with those 'screened-in' transported to the mainland and others returned to Haiti. When court injunctions temporarily prevented returns at the end of 1991 (Ghezelbash, 2018), Guantanamo Bay was used as a holding and processing centre, though screening was suspended in May 1992 when the US disclaimed non-refoulement responsibilities – a position later upheld (though widely condemned) by the Supreme Court in Sale (Sale v Haitian Centers Council, 509 US 155 (1993)). Some form of screening has been re-introduced a number of times over the years, with several Caribbean states used for processing and resettling those recognised as refugees. As of 2017, Guantanamo Bay has no longer been in use as a holding facility, though the possibility of reviving this usage has been a focus for more recent discussion (Amnesty International, 2022)

Moreno-Lax (2021) also outlines an 'indirect' form of interdiction, which does not require full-contact but is conducted 'from a distance' by escorting vessels out of jurisdiction, enlisting the support of third parties, or deflecting responsibility onto third countries, even without their consent. She gives the example of the *Tampa* case in which a Norwegian registered container ship carrying 433 rescued asylum seekers was refused permission to disembark on Christmas Island (part of Australia), being technically in the Search and Rescue Region of Indonesia. The asylum seekers were eventually transferred to Nauru and New Zealand for status determination, and thereafter Australia excised all territories outside the mainland from the 'migration zone', such that Australian legislation (including status determination) no longer applied (Ghezelbash, 2018). There have also been reports of push-backs into Indonesian waters and handovers to Sri Lankan authorities in a 'stop the boats' approach thinly disguised as rescue (Moreno-Lax, 2021). A policy emerged whereby all unauthorised arrivals would be transferred to Nauru or Papua New Guinea[2] for processing and (if recognised) settlement there or in a third country. The detail of this policy has gone through various shifts (see Ghezelbash, 2018; Johnson, [2014] 2018) but the dominant message has been that no-one entering irregularly will ever be given the opportunity to settle in Australia. Status determination was therefore to take place under the law and jurisdiction of the deciding country, with only offshore applications having any prospect of full (CSR) recognition. Britain has meanwhile been striving to bypass judicial scrutiny of an arrangement with Rwanda for the processing and management of irregular arrivals on British shores (as discussed later in this chapter).

Arrangements to shift control of asylum applications to third countries by excising parts of national territory and/or shifting migration control into the territory or territorial waters of another state has been described by Gammeltoft-Hansen (2011) as a growing commercialisation of sovereignty. Among states that have bartered migration management in this way he lists Spain, which holds agreements with Senegal and Mauritania to intercept and return irregular migrants in their waters, and Italy, which holds agreements with Libya. A British policy of pushback to France was withdrawn in April 2022 in the face of an upcoming Judicial Review (BBC.co, 2022). However, a summit in March 2023 led to agreement that Britain would fund additional French border guards and detention facilities in what amounts to a contractual agreement on 'pullback'. French maritime police have been recorded using dangerous methods to turn boats heading into the Channel (Observer, 2024a), and there have also been several failures on the part of the UK coastguard to respond to vessels in distress in British waters (Observer, 2023).

A recent report (Farahat and Markard, 2020:10) on the growing trend of active evasion of search and rescue observes that

> in order to avoid responsibility for migrants in distress at sea, EU member States are seeking to outsource it to third countries in Northern Africa, by disembarking rescued migrants there, by directing private shipmasters to do so, or by calling on Northern African authorities.

The report also notes that Libya 'most certainly', but also Algeria, Egypt, Morroco and Tunisia cannot be considered places of safety for asylum seekers and that instructions to shipmasters to carry out disembarkations there do not excuse the destination state from international responsibility.

---

2 Papua New Guinea until 2021 only.

Moreno-Lax (2021) also shows how interdiction can be accomplished 'by omission', especially in the Mediterranean, when migrants deaths are an accepted outcome of controls that include a negation or criminalisation of rescue, and even outright abandonment of vessels. There have been reports of the Libyan coastguard interfering with humanitarian rescue attempts (Guardian, 2024) as well as coerced recruitment of arrivals in Greece to engage in the unlawful removal of others back to Turkey (Guardian, 2022b). In the case of Hirsi Jamaa and Others (Grande Chamber 2012), Italy was condemned by the European Court of Human Rights (ECtHR) for the interdiction and return of 'boat migrants', in a ruling that deemed push-backs to Libya to be a form of collective expulsion and ill-treatment, and also clarified the extra-territorial purchase of non-refoulement. Italy had presented the push-back to Libya simply as a refusal of entry, but the court emphasised that the CSR is a living instrument, to be interpreted in the light of present conditions, and that its guarantees must be practical and effective.

However, interdiction by omission can also apply in the absence of direct engagement when naval assets have been withdrawn from rescue endeavours (regarded as 'pull factors'), and drones are used instead to capture information while avoiding direct contact with vessels that might be in distress (Moreno-Lax, 2021). The use of private agencies or third-party organisations can also inhibit accountability, and a recent case before the European Court of Justice dismissed the claim of a Syrian man who had arrived on the Greek island of Milos by boat and on transfer to Leros expressed a desire to seek international protection. In a joint operation by Frontex and Greece, the man and his family were transferred to Turkey, and thence to Iraq, but claimed they had been subject to a push-back whereby Frontex had breached the rules on asylum procedure. The court, however, ruled that Frontex was tasked with providing technical and operational support to member states, and that member states alone are competent to assess return decisions (Guardian, 2023d), thus rendering Frontex unaccountable.

In reviewing the range of interdiction strategies, Moreno-Lax (2021:500) concludes that 'the precise modalities are varied and can range from forms of 'direct', 'indirect' and 'by omission' interdiction employed to deflect responsibilities onto third countries or to neglect them altogether'. The few examples outlined above, in fact amount to stratified access to status determination, ranging from collective repulsion (push-back) without individual examination, through return to a point of departure on the basis of summary screening, to extra-territorial processing under the jurisdiction of an offshore country, and extra-territorial processing under the jurisdiction of the intercepting authority. All stand as efforts to evade direct responsibility for determining status and supporting asylum seekers on a national territory that has nevertheless accepted all of the obligations contained in the CSR. We also see the shift in emphasis observed by Johnson [2014] (2018) away from the distinction between forced and voluntary migration towards that of mode of entry – irregularity is now the focus of heightened concern and attention, while extra-territorial processing and privatisation of control are described by Gammeltoft-Hansen (2011) as a retreat of the state that creates a growing legal black hole.

The complexities of interdiction and offshoring have contributed to the fragmentation of protected status that Zetter (2007) refers to, in that outcomes can vary according to the country overseeing the process and can also change over time as the detail of policy shifts. To take Australia as an example, outcomes were made much more complex by the use of offshoring and have included full (CSR) recognition but settlement in a third country only, Temporary Protection Visas on Australian soil (no longer in use), Permanent Protection Status that falls short of full recognition, a bridging visa to accommodate temporary transfer from offshore sites to the mainland, or denial of status and removal. Meanwhile, Britain has been moving towards an offshoring arrangement with Rwanda, and should this go ahead, a similar array of outcomes is likely as full (CSR) recognition and settlement in Britain becomes vanishingly rare, and lawful entry to Britain for the purposes of seeking asylum is being defined out of existence. CSR recognition offshore will be for settlement in a third country, as will the slightly lesser humanitarian protection under the European Convention on Human Rights, for those who do not meet the CSR grounds of persecution (No Recourse to Public Funds (NRPF), 2023). Resettlement in Britain would therefore be reserved for recognised refugees selected from UNHCR camps, while others for whom a third country destination is not viable seem likely to be confined to a form of legal limbo. We look more closely at the unfolding of this picture in Britain later in this chapter.

Holding spaces, camps and basic maintenance

Given a growing shift in emphasis towards offshoring as a means of containing irregular entry and stay, questions inevitably arise about the treatment of, and provision for, those who are awaiting an outcome of their applications for protection – as well as those whose application has been refused. In fact the variety of 'holding' spaces for people caught up in the different stages of a search for protection seems in itself to amount to a stratified system of maintenance and stay, with shifting terms and conditions of treatment. Guantanamo Bay has featured as a holding space for asylum seekers taken up from vessels seeking entry to the US, while Australia has for many years applied a policy of mandatory detention for asylum seekers, largely situated in offshore locations. In both cases Ghezelbash (2018) has argued that the determination procedure was faulty by virtue of a failure to provide legal assistance to detainees or opportunities for appeal, and a failure to consider complementary protection.

Detention facilities of this kind have sometimes been referred to as camps in Agamben's sense (as noted by Johnson, [2014] 2018:127), that is spaces of exception specifically designed to lie outside of legal control, though in practice there is considerable variety within and between such facilities, which are not entirely sealed off from the rule of law. Conditions in Guantanamo Bay were improved over time (Ghezelbash, 2018:154) but it has not been used to house asylum seekers since 2017; detention on Manus Island was found to be unconstitutional by the Supreme Court of Papua New Guinea and the centre was forcibly closed in 2017. After long-running reports of neglect and abuse, the last detainee was scheduled to leave Nauru in July of 2023 (Straits Times, 2023), though Australia plans to retain an offshore detention capacity on the island indefinitely (Guardian, 2021; BBC.com, 2023). There has been considerable criticism of the conditions on both Nauru and in the Manus Island centre, with problems variously related to overcrowding, exposure to the elements, insufficient drinking water, food and sanitation, and reports of suicide, self-harm, and assault (Ghezelbash, 2018). Though the detention facilities have been run down and there are now very few arrivals on Australian territory, critics argue that this is not a mark of success for deterrent policy but rather a feature of interception and push-backs by the navy.

It is significant that Britain has been preparing the way for more expansive powers of detention and reduced judicial oversight as the 2023 Illegal Migration Act (discussed below) comes into force, an act that also establishes a number of measures to contain and deter irregular entry. Among other things, the Act amends existing legislation to replace two key principles: that detention may only be for a period that is reasonable, and if removal is not to take place within a reasonable period then detention powers should not be exercised (Section 12). The decision on what is a reasonable period of detention will then rest with the Secretary of State, and directions for removal can take as long as he/she deems necessary.

This legislation came into force just after a public inquiry into abuse at a UK detention centre made its report (Guardian, 2023) and in so doing identified numerous breaches of human rights laws relating to torture and inhuman and degrading treatment. The report speaks of a toxic culture that is manifest in racist and derogatory language, repeated use of inherently dangerous restraint techniques, forcible movement of men when naked or near naked, and inappropriate and intimidating use of riot shields and balaclavas. The Chair of the inquiry, Kate Eves, observed that it had identified wholescale failures in the application of safeguarding rules and the creation of an environment in which unacceptable treatment was more likely to flourish. The relevant press report notes that 'it also raises questions about the viability of the Home Office's policies to expand immigration detention tenfold, especially for asylum seekers'.

Detention facilities assume greater significance in relation to asylum where they are used not simply for the timely removal of failed applicants but also for pending claims to be considered by a third country in offshore arrangements for transferring this responsibility. They sit on a continuum with other holding spaces, or 'camps', that correspond more closely to the literal meaning of this word, and spring up in a more or less spontaneous manner under very particular circumstances. One such was known as the Calais jungle, which existed for most of 2016, made up of people – including unaccompanied minors – seeking unauthorised entry to Britain. The conditions, on occasion termed a 'living hell', were 'so bad that describing them cannot capture the squalor. You have to smell conditions like these and feel the squelch of mud mixed with urine and much else…to feel the horror' (ZAT and Ors v SSHD [2016] EWCA Civ 810 para 23). The camp was demolished on October of 2016 and such sites tend to have only temporary existence, but other camps have also established themselves at critical border sites, as for example the heavily forti-fied zone between Morroco and the Spanish enclave of Melilla. An estimated 1500 migrants – many of them asylum seekers – gathered in woodlands in the region, and following frequent attacks on make-shift camps, made an attempt to storm the border fences in June of 2022, which met with brutal physical violence from Morrocan agents and Spanish police. Such spontaneous clus-ters are portrayed by Johnson [2014] (2018) as manifestations of 'migrant agency' at the borders of Europe, an insistence on 'the making and remaking of one's own life on the scenery of the world' (p.160), but the human cost is high and the odds are stacked against success.

Other holding spaces take a more formal guise and serve as waiting rooms overseen by the UNHCR, from which a fortunate few are selected for resettle-ment, constituting the principle example of the promised safe and legal chan-nels, ostensibly serving to compensate for restrictive controls. These camps are intended as temporary solutions for people forced to flee their homes, but in cases of long-term displacement, they can become semi-permanent set-tlements that must therefore secure the provision of basic services, includ-ing education. Colin Yeo (2022:258) writes 'Many millions of refugees find themselves warehoused for years in refugee camps, where multiple genera-tions are unable to work and are denied many of the minimum rights of a normal human life'. He goes on to state that only ten countries host 65% of the world's refugees, 86% being in the global south. A small number of refugees from such camps will be chosen for resettlement in countries of the global north, where if and when this happens they move to perhaps the most privi-leged position in terms of the hierarchy of asylum, in that their path to settled living in the host country is to some extent smoothed by assistance and advice. However, although in 2019 the UNHCR identified 1.4 million people in need of resettlement, many of these will never be successfully submitted. In 2018, for example, 81,000 were submitted and 56,000 were eventually resettled. 'This means that in 2018, approximately 5% of those in need of resettlement (estimated at 1.2 million by UNHCR) actually achieved this end' (Wilkins, 2020). So in terms of a stratified system, the extremes of the spectrum go from the spontaneous camps that emerge in border hot-spots, through to detention either pre- or post-status determination, and on to the formal 'waiting-room' camps under UNHCR authority. The arrangements of any given 'host' country will sit in shifting relationship to these contextual structures, and given this background we can now turn to the classification, stratification and control of asylum in the particular case of the UK.

Classifying and stratifying – Maintenance, deterrence and survival

This section will cover the key features of what could be seen as the contemporary era of asylum in Britain, which began with the significant rise in numbers of applications to 26,205 in 1990 – a step change from the 4,389 applications received in 1985. Numbers fluctuated in the 1990s from around 25,000 to around 45,000 to then reach their highest level of 84,130 in 2002 (Select Committee on Home Affairs, 2004), and after falling to a twenty-year low of 17,916 in 2010, they peaked again at 81,130 in 2022 (Sturge, 2023). Despite changes of the government and party in power at key points, much of the period since 1990 to the present has been characterised by policies intended to deter people from seeking asylum in Britain, which have grown ever more extreme in their design and effects. The classification and stratification of status and rights have been a dominant feature of these manoeuvres, and an early measure introduced in 1996 – just as applications had neared 44,000 – turned on mode of entry. A key device was the distinction between those making their claims 'at port', and those who waited until after entry to the territory to claim 'in country', so the policy, in effect, created two categories of asylum seekers, one of which was to be stripped of eligibility for support.

Maintenance provision is regarded as necessary to make a right to seek asylum meaningful, but the policy rationale was that in-county claimants had entered the country in some other capacity and on the basis of no recourse to public funds. They should not therefore come into eligibility for support simply by making an asylum claim – though the asylum application would itself be given due consideration. The argument that characterised the times was a claim that a majority of asylum seekers were 'bogus', that is not genuinely fleeing persecution, but in fact were economic migrants attracted by the benefits system, and hence: 'that can't be right and we're going to stop it' (Social Security Committee, 1996). The focus was on the 70% of applicants who claimed asylum having entered the country in some other capacity, and who were therefore viewed as less likely to be 'genuine' refugees, but as with later deterrent measures, there was no attempt to distinguish between the genuine and non-genuine, and the policies at issue were not designed to do so. Perhaps the most interesting aspect of this particular policy is that there were three different attempts to make it work, each one knocked back by legal challenge. The first attempt (under a Conservative government) was deemed *ultra vires* by virtue of its confinement to secondary legislation, and the second attempt (later in 1996) was rendered ineffective by the ruling that in-country asylum seekers were eligible for local authority support, being 'in need of care and attention' under the 1948 National Assistance Act. The third attempt (in 2002) – by then under a Labour government – was deemed a breach of the guarantee of protection from inhuman and degrading treatment, article 3 of the European Convention on Human Rights, and hence the Human Rights Act (for a more detailed history see Morris, 2010).

A further element of stratification had been built into maintenance support as of 1999, when the level of maintenance paid to asylum seekers was reduced from 90 per cent of mainstream benefit levels[3] to 70 per cent on the assumption that higher rates were attracting 'non-genuine' claims (Home Affairs Committee, 2013). The form of support was also changed with the National Asylum Support System that introduced compulsory dispersal, supposedly to distribute asylum seekers more evenly between local authorities. However, in some areas there were concentrations well above the recommended level, as in deprived locations where cheaper housing was available – often from private providers under squalid conditions – but also exposing asylum seekers to resentment and stigma from local populations who were themselves struggling economically (BBC.co, 2016). Since then other erosions have unfolded, as when an uprating link to mainstream benefits was broken in 2008 to be later followed by a freezing of rates in 2011, justified by the assertion that increased rates would 'clog up the system' with spurious claims (BBC.co, 2014). In 2015 preferential rates for children were removed as a means of discouraging parents from 'economic migration' (Ghulam and Ors v SSHD [2016] EWHC 2639 (Admin), para 241). There are, however, limits to how low the level of provision can sink, and in December 2022 the High Court made a mandatory order requiring an uplift of maintenance payments to £45 per week, in order properly to take account of inflation (R(CB) v SSHD [2022] EWHC 3329 (Admin)).

However, a lower level within this stratified system applies to failed asylum seekers without children, whose circumstances (usually the barriers to their removal) mean they must be offered support. When asylum support *via* a short-lived voucher system was abandoned in the face of a human rights challenge, vouchers were retained for failed asylum seekers (section 4 support under 1999 Act), to be later replaced with a pre-payment card. Conditions for receipt have been heightened and the onus of proof regarding barriers to departure has shifted from the Home Office to the applicant, driving some failed asylum seekers 'underground' to the extremes of destitution and despair (See Jesuit Refugee Services, 2018).

---

3 The lower rate of 90% was justified by being of likely shorter duration for asylum seekers.

Accommodation for asylum seekers can also be viewed in terms of a stratified system, which – as noted above – really starts with the informal camps that spring up at key border points, the more formal UNHCR 'waiting room' camps, and the growing use of detention in the early stages of a claim. This was especially the case with respect to a 'detained fast-track' system introduced in 2003 for claims that were considered suitable for a quick decision, though the selection was made on the basis of very little information and 99 per cent of such claims were refused (Guardian, 2022). In 2015 the Court of Appeal (The Lord Chancellor v Detention Action [2015] EWCA Civ 840) found the system to be structurally unfair and unjust, and therefore *ultra vires*. Plans to re-introduce fast-tracking detention would seem to have been superseded by the 2023 Illegal Migration Act, discussed below. The next rung on the ladder in terms of accommodation might be reception centres, though local resistance prevented their introduction as the favoured approach in Britain in 2002 (Home Office, 2002). This 'managed accommodation' was argued to promise 'end-to end credibility' for the system, by combining induction, housing, maintenance and reporting, leading to integration or removal. Such an approach has seen a recent revival with the use of a 'detention like' facility at Napier barracks, lodging single men in dormitory style accommodation with inadequate facilities, behind barbed wire and padlocked gates. The use of the barracks was later ruled unlawful, though not necessarily beyond improvement (NB and Ors v SSHD [2021] EWHC 1489 (Admin)), but since then a further questionable form of accommodation has raised concern. The Bibby Stockholm barge, described by the inmates as 'unsafe, frightening and isolated' and a 'place of exile', was temporarily evacuated on the discovery of legionella bacteria (Guardian, 2023a), but continued refusal of the accommodation will mean a disqualification from support. Two Royal Air Force barracks are also being called into use for accommodation that seems to sit somewhere between detention and reception, while a crisis has arisen over the use of hotel accommodation for unaccompanied minors, ruled unlawful under the 1989 Children Act (ECPAT UK v Kent County Council and SSHD [2023] EWHC 1953 (Admin)). These crises are symptomatic of a continuing belief in 'deterrence' as a means of control, a growing failure to address the needs of asylum seekers, and currently a very considerable backlog of people awaiting a decision on their claim. However, this history has also been a prelude to more extreme measures that are now being rolled out to dramatically reduce the presence of asylum seekers in Britain.

The Nationality and Borders Act (2022)

Britain's Nationality and Borders Act (NABA) of 2022 prepared the way for processing asylum claims outside the UK (along the lines of the Australian model) as the political rhetoric on 'stop the boats' has achieved ever greater prominence. Of the six principle source countries (Afghanistan, India, Iran,

Iraq, Syria and Eritrea), five have a very high chance of their claims being recognised, and the Refugee Council has calculated that 74 per cent of small boat arrivals from January to October 2023 would be granted recognition (Refugee Council, 2023). The rise in small boat arrivals in 2021 and 2022 nevertheless provoked a reaction of panic from the government, although the real numbers problem (insofar as there is one) stems from the tens of thousands who have been waiting for a decision for more than one year, with 175,000 undecided cases as of August 2023 (Guardian, 2023b). It is worth noting here that despite an increase of asylum seekers held in detention, removals and voluntary departures show a decline (Yeo, 2023).

Though much of NABA, 2022 has been rendered largely redundant by the Illegal Migration Act of 2023, its key measures are of interest for this chapter as they introduced a new element to the classification of claimants (see Webber, 2022; Migration Yorkshire, 2022) – the main distinction being between arrivals with a visa, including those from a recognised resettlement scheme, and those without a visa. Arrivals in the latter category are criminalised by the Act (as are humanitarian volunteers) and will immediately be liable to a four-year prison sentence, though it is well known that there is no visa that accommodates the intent to seek asylum. Furthermore, those asylum seekers who do not arrive directly from the country they are fleeing, or who have a 'connection' with a safe third country, will be deemed 'inadmissible', to be housed in barracks or similar accommodation (Reception Centres) for six months as the government seeks their removal to a 'safe' third country. Should this not prove possible their claims would be processed and those recognised as refugees (under the CSR) would receive 30 months (renewable) leave to remain, a reduced right to family reunification, no welfare eligibility and the prospect of removal thereafter. The act therefore appears to yield four different categories (albeit with some overlap) – those removed as unlawful entrants without a consideration of their case (to be processed elsewhere), those inadmissible (indirect) arrivals processed and recognised in Britain but granted only temporary stay, those 'admissible' asylum seekers granted full recognition, and those recognised and resettled under an established scheme. These are in addition to 'failed' asylum seekers who have been processed and rejected, though it seems that in practice the third group (admissible and recognised) will be all but defined out of existence.

The Act also raises the standard of proof required for a successful claim, reinstates fast-track appeals (despite the *ultra vires* ruling on a previous detained-fast-track route), and legislates for the use of offshore processing, the latter to deal with unlawful entrants and 'inadmissible' claims. However, Home Office guidance confirms that unaccompanied minors are not suitable for the inadmissibility process, and that families with children must be treated with due regard to statutory provisions on the child's best interests – a provision now overridden in the 2023 Act. NABA also raises the threshold for 'reasonable grounds' decisions that grant access to support for potential victims of trafficking under the National Referral Mechanism, and downgrades the leave associated with humanitarian protection from 5 years, with access to public funds, to a ten year wait before possible settlement and no welfare support (NRPF, 2022). The highly respected NGO No Recourse to Public Funds (NRPF) has expressed concern that the changes could lead to more people falling into destitution, and for families with children this could mean responsibility devolves to the local authority.

Closely allied to the NABA 2022 is the UK-Rwanda migration and economic development partnership, announced on 14 April 2022 (Blake, 2022). Though in theory the 2022 Act delivers four categories of asylum seeker, these categories can be collapsed into a two tier system based on mode of arrival in Britain: Group 1 refugees were to receive leave to remain for five years and can then apply for ILR. They have family unification rights, access to public funds and a right to work. Group 2 claimants (the inadmissible group) were to be considered for removal to a safe third country – more specifically transfer to Rwanda, for a consideration of their case. If such a transfer (to Rwanda or elsewhere) could not be completed the case was to be considered in Britain and if recognised granted the lesser array of rights detailed above.

There is one other aspect of the NABA 2022 that might be construed as stratifying in its effects, and that is the purchase of article 31 of the CSR, which provides that refugees should not have any penalties imposed on them as a consequence of illegally entering or being present in the country of refuge in order to seek sanctuary. This protection holds provided that they travelled directly from the country where they fear persecution and presented themselves without delay, while also showing good cause for their illegal entry or presence. How this should be applied is not self-evident, however, and Section 37 of the NABA aims to limit the application of article 31 where an asylum seeker stopped in a safe third country and is unable show that they could not reasonably have made a claim for asylum, or where they made their UK claim after their presence became unlawful. Furthermore, if someone should enter on a tourist (or other) visa and then apply for asylum this would not in itself be a breach of Section 40 of NABA, which defines illegal entry, but it could be construed as the use of deception when applying for a visa. As a result it is almost impossible to lawfully enter the UK in order to claim asylum and the protection offered by article 31 has therefore been tightly constrained by NABA, to apply only to the narrow (or non-existent) group of refugees who cannot be deemed inadmissible.

Finally, much of the viability of the NABA 2022 rested on the feasibility of the Rwanda plan, and in December of 2022 the High Court (AAA and Ors v SSHD [2022] EWHC 3230 (Admin)) found in favour of the government in a challenge from eight asylum seekers awaiting removal to Rwanda. However, the decision was later reversed by the Court of Appeal (AAA and Ors v SSHD [2023] EWCA Civ 745); the policy itself was not considered to be unlawful by the court, but it was ruled that removals to Rwanda could not go ahead unless a number of deficiencies were corrected. A decision from the Supreme Court was still pending (though later found against the government – AAA and Ors v SSHD [2023] UKSC 42) when the configuration of asylum law was altered yet again by the 2023 Illegal Migration Act, which passed into law on 20 July 2023.

The Illegal Migration Act 2023

There is an irony in the title of this act, in that many of its critics have argued that the act itself is unlawful; going further than its predecessor (NABA, 2022) it erases the differentiated status for recognised refugees but in doing so adopts an even more intransigent approach. The earlier act left open the possibility of a ten year route to settlement for those whose applications would have been deemed inadmissible in the event of a third country accepting their transfer. Those already placed on this route are now to have their conditions aligned to 'Group 1' refugees, but as the Government Factsheet tells us:

> The Illegal Migration Bill [now act] will change the law to make it unambiguously clear that if you enter the UK illegally, you should not be able to remain here. Instead, you will be detained and promptly removed either to your home country or to a safe country where any asylum claim will be considered…the only way to come to the UK for asylum will be through safe and legal routes.
>
> (GOV.UK, 2023)

In effect, no asylum seeker entering unlawfully would ever in the future be given permission to stay and could never be lawfully joined by their family (unless they enter under some other status), so the two-tier system introduced in NABA 2022 would then entail a simpler and harsher binary divide, as the compromise measure of the ten-year route is abolished. However, the implementation of the law threatens to create a much larger group who are present but without status and having no prospect of a change in their circumstances are in effect in limbo. The Act imposes a duty on the Home Secretary to remove asylum seekers and others who enter the UK in breach of immigration laws, and unless safe third country destinations become available, there would very soon be large numbers of asylum seekers present without status, whom the Home Secretary is obliged but unable to remove. The duty does not apply to children while they remain children but will do so as soon as they reach 18.

There is also a new wide power to detain under the Act, including families with children and unaccompanied minors, and existing safeguards for the latter are dis-applied. So in effect, the legilsation creates a realistic prospect of tens of thousands of asylum seekers who cannot be removed and for whom there is insufficient detention capacity, being released on bail with no right to work, entitled to state support, and with no route to refugee status. The denial of such people ever achieving a right of residence also means that should they have children born in Britain they will not be born British citizens, while the duty to remove, power to detain and ban on ever being granted status will also apply to victims of modern slavery. One commentator's conclusion on the act is:

> For the government it looks disastrous. It is a disaster if removals to a safe country like Rwanda do become possible. It is also a disaster if they don't…In recent years enforced removals of failed asylum seekers have virtually ceased. Just 489 failed asylum seekers were removed in the year ending September 2022.
>
> (Yeo, 2023a)

So where will all these people go?

Again we come to the viability of the Rwanda agreement, which has been delayed by a legal challenge and the differing judicial opinions that have followed (Pennington, 2023). A challenge mounted by Asylum Aid and ten asylum seekers raised the following issues: the weight to be given to diplomatic assurances; the relevance of formal and informal reporting mechanisms; and the risk of removal of failed asylum seekers from Rwanda to face persecution. The High Court (AAA and Ors v SSHD [2022] EWHC 3230 (Admin)) and later the Lord Chief Justice in the Court of Appeal accepted the governments' case in response, but the majority in the subsequent Court of Appeal hearing (the Master of the Rolls, and LJ Underhill – AAA and Ors v SSHD [2023] EWCA Civ 745) were not convinced of the robustness of the system. A further significant point was made by LJ Underhill, who stated that the penalties referred to under article 31 of the CSR are not confined to criminal sanctions and could include obstruction of access to status determination, which echoes the point about stratified effects made above. Since the Appeal Court ruling the Supreme Court (AAA and Ors v SSHD [2023] UKSC 42) has determined that there are substantial grounds for believing that the removal of any asylum seeker to Rwanda under the terms of the Migration and Economic and Development Partnership between the governments of Rwanda and the United Kingdom would breach the principle of non-refoulement. In response the British government set about passing legislation that will declare Rwanda safe, though at the same time it has been revealed that the Home Office granted refugee status to four Rwandan's showing well-founded fears of persecution in their home country, one of them on the very day the government concluded the Supreme Court case, arguing that Rwanda is a safe country (Observer, 2024). Furthermore, the Safety of Rwanda (Immigration and Asylum) Bill has been found by the Joint Committee on Human Rights (2024) to be incompatible with the UK's human rights obligations, to erode the protections laid down by the HRA and to fall short of various international treaties. Not least, it seeks to override the ruling from the Supreme Court and to establish near total exclusion of judicial scrutiny. The ultimate outcome is now placed in question by the forthcoming general election (of July, 2024).

Whatever the final fate of the Rwandan partnership, the other area of weakness in the whole policy position is the limited availability of safe and legal routes to access asylum. As mentioned earlier, the UNHCR camps are in effect huge warehousing spaces where people wait and hope for resettlement, and the host countries are in a position to both determine the numbers they accept and (within limits) to specify their characteristics. Although the government factsheet claims that addressing 'illegal' migration will release greater capacity to provide a safe haven through resettlement schemes, the progress to date falls far short of compensating for the numbers that risk their lives in small boat crossings. Resettled refugees totalled less than 2000 in 2021, the most numerous year to date, as compared to 4,548 crossings from January to March 2022 (Lenegan, 2023). Those who are selected and resettled are a relatively privileged group, accounting for only 1% of refugees worldwide (Solf and Rehgber, 2021) and in Britain they have a smoother experience than 'spontaneous' applicants in terms of their transition to settled status, which filters through to a stratified reception system and provides easier access to mainstream services. The issue has been subject to critical comment from the All Party Parliamentary Group (APPG) (2017) who reported that resettled refugees are better supported in accessing mainstream benefits and the labour market, while 'spontaneous' arrivals suffer a serious deficit. Other schemes, not strictly speaking 'refugee' schemes in the CSR sense, have included the Afghan Relocation and Assistance scheme which evacuated around 15,000 people in 2021, and the Ukrainian sponsorship scheme that covered 120,000 Ukrainians. However, homelessness is currently a significant and growing problem for the latter group as the sponsorship arrangements draw to a close, but nor is the problem of homelessness confined to this group. Allied to an attempt to address the backlog of pending asylum decisions, the notice of removal from asylum accommodation has been cut from 28 to seven days, with charities warning that 'camps' of the homeless will spring up in cities – and these will be refugees with CSR recognition (Guardian, 2023c).

In sum, the 2023 Act seeks to usher in a new regime that is ethically questionable, and for which the most critical pieces are not yet in place, though there are reasons to doubt if they ever will be. While a form of stratification is apparent in terms of differential access to procedure and rights, and varying degrees of neglect in terms of maintenance and survival, it seems to lack any rationale with respect to who is hardest hit – the only driving justification being indiscriminate deterrence.

Moral standing

Throughout this chapter we have seen examples of how the stratification of rights operates in the context of asylum, ranging from variable access to status determination, through different types of accommodation and maintenance arrangements, varying degrees of recognition and protection, and finally different modes of entry and entitlement. It is the last of these issues that points most clearly to what Johnson [2014] (2018) refers to as a new paradigm for the emergent global refugee regime – one that is fully apparent in Britain – and that is the shift from viewing asylum seeking as a form of forced migration to seeing it predominantly through the lens of irregularity. This shift is driven by the primacy that sovereign states place on control, and its pejorative implications are readily apparent, encouraging an association between asylum seeking and illegality (as in the 2023 act in Britain), and enabling distinctions of worth to be made on this basis. Hence, Boris Johnson's comment 'If you come here illegally you are illegal migrants...and the law will treat you as such',[4] or Teresa May's (2015) distinction between 'the wealthiest, luckiest and strongest' who make spontaneous (uncontrolled) claims after 'abusing the system',[5] as against the vulnerable groups admitted under the UK's Syrian Vulnerable Persons Resettlement Scheme (now closed). The supporting rationale rests on a discourse of abuse, which draws boundaries of desert and distinctions of worth based on mode of arrival – and a recent example sees the then Home Secretary claiming that: '70% of individuals on small boats are single men who are effectively economic migrants', when in fact the rate of recognition for small boat arrivals would be 74% (Guardian, 2023e)

The intended effect is an erosion of what Lockwood terms 'moral resources', which drive informal distinctions of gain or deficit in the functioning of a regime of rights – so while the right to seek asylum is notionally intact there is a deficit in its operation according to ease of access to status determination and the stigma increasingly attached to the label of asylum seeker. As much as twenty years ago Britain's Press Complaints Commission (PCC), in October 2003, issued a guidance note that stated: 'As an asylum seeker is someone currently seeking refugee status or humanitarian protection, there can be no such thing in law as an 'illegal asylum seeker' (Guardian, 2003), and yet we now have an 'Illegal Migration Act' that is directly aimed at asylum seekers. The note goes on to observe that the Press Complaints Commission (PCC) Code of Practice: 'has underlined the danger that inaccurate, misleading or distorted reporting may generate an atmosphere of fear and hostility that is not borne out by the facts'. But in practice what we find is the systematic use of pejorative comments and questionable associations to undermine the public perceptions of asylum seekers as a prelude to shrinking their rights. We saw this process in operation in the at port/in country distinction, whereby the latter group was viewed as non-genuine refugees, attracted by the availability of benefits, we see it in the distinction between spontaneous

---

4 ITV News on X: https://t.co/rkUOx1VcdR https://t.co/lD4rTN6V4p" / X (twitter.com).
5 For 2012–16 the latter outnumbered the former by 5:1 (APPG, 2017).

and resettled asylum seekers, and we see it in the elision between irregular entry and illegality.

We have noted in previous chapters that moral standing features not simply in the erosion of rights, but also in relation to attempts to combat such erosion through civic activism. This is what Lockwood terms civic expansion, and it is also apparent in the argument from Habermas (1996) that the role of civil society is to bring matters of import from the periphery to the centre of public concern. However, where public sympathy is lacking or needs to be built, activists may take their concerns to the courts, and we have seen examples in relation to the removal of welfare support for in-country claimants (Adam, Limbuela and Tesema v SSHD [2005] United Kingdom House of Lords (UKHL) 66), and in the challenge to British policy aimed at 'offshoring' claims to Rwanda (AAA (Syria) and Ors v SSHD [2023] UKSC 42). The question remains of how far success in these fora can help to restore the moral standing of the target group, but the overall configuration yields a theory of change that passes through a number of stages.

Firstly comes the fact that the complex of rights is open to manipulation and change by the state, then secondly that there is scope for a link between formal entitlement and informal status, or moral standing. These elements combine to yield the possibility that possession of moral resources can lead to an enhancement of rights, or correspondingly that the possession of rights itself confers a degree of moral standing; but the reverse also applies, such that an attack on moral standing can serve as a prelude to the diminution of rights. We have seen this dynamic in play in relation to civic stratification and asylum – it is what Zetter (2007:174) had in mind when he wrote of politicised labels and the transformation of identities to fit populist images, or what Yeo (2020) means when he refers to the role of deterrence in reassuring the public. It is a dynamic that is also captured by Fassin (2009:15) when he refers to the mental state of a community being historically created, modified and destroyed – civic stratification is a crucial tool for understanding how this comes about.

References

Amnesty International (2022) USA: Biden administration must not detain Haitian asylum seekers at Guantánamo – Amnesty International 1 November (accessed 27.2.24)

Arendt, H. [1948] (1979) *The Origins of Totalitarianism*, New York: Harcourt Brace

BBC.co (2014) Theresa May defeated over asylum seeker benefits – BBC News 9 April (accessed 4.3.24)

BBC.co (2016) 'Impending shortage' of asylum seeker homes in the UK – BBC News 4 March (accessed 28.2.24)

BBC.co (2022) Channel migrant boats: Ministers drop plans to turn back vessels – BBC News 26 April (accessed 13.3.24)

BBC.co (2023) Nauru: Why Australia is funding an empty detention centre – BBC News 8 July (accessed 28.2.24)

Blake, H. (2022) Rwanda and refugee rights: Six things to know about the Nationality and Borders Act | The Law Society 11 May (accessed 1.3.24)

Farahat, A. and N. Markard (2020) *Places of Safety in the Mediterranean: The EU's Policy of Outsourcing Responsiblity,* Brussels: Heinrich Boll Stiftung

Fassin, D. (2009) 'Moral economies revisited' *Annales, Histoire, Sciences Sociales* 64(6):1237

Gammeltoft-Hansen, T. (2011) *Access to Asylum,* Cambridge University Press

Ghezelbash, D. (2018) *Refuge Lost,* Cambridge: Cambridge University Press

GOV.UK (2023) Illegal migration bill: Overarching factsheet – GOV.UK (www.gov.uk) 20 July (accessed 1.3.24)

The Guardian (2003) PCC acts on asylum seekers | UK news | The Guardian 23 October (accessed 4.3.24)

The Guardian (2021) Australia signs deal with Nauru to keep asylum seeker detention centre open indefinitely | Australian immigration and asylum | The Guardian 24 September (accessed 28.2.24)

The Guardian (2022) Labour wants to fast-track asylum cases from 'safe' countries to clear backlog | Immigration and asylum | The Guardian 9 December (accessed 1.3.24)

The Guardian (2022a) A timeline of migrant channel crossing deaths since 2019 | Immigration and asylum | The Guardian 14 December (accessed 14.3.24)

The Guardian (2022b) Revealed: Greek police coerce asylum seekers into pushing fellow migrants back to Turkey | Migration and development | The Guardian 28 June (accessed 19.3.24)

The Guardian (2023) Physical and verbal abuse found in Brook House immigration removal centre inquiry | Immigration and asylum | The Guardian 19 September (accessed 28.2.24)

The Guardian (2023a) Braverman's plan to house UK asylum seekers on 'deathtrap' barge faces legal hurdle | Immigration and asylum | The Guardian 27 August (accessed 1.3.24)

The Guardian (2023b) UK asylum backlog hits record high as over 175,000 await decision | Immigration and asylum | The Guardian 24 August (accessed 1.3.24)

The Guardian (2023c) Dire warning of refugee 'camps' crisis after eviction notice is cut, 4 October, p.15

The Guardian (2023d) 'It was horrible': Syrian man deported from Greece tells of family's trauma | Refugees | The Guardian 6 September (accessed 13.3.24)

The Guardian (2023e) Charity challenges home secretary's claims about 'economic migrants' | Suella Braverman | The Guardian 2 October (accessed 4.3.24)

The Guardian (2024) Libya coastguard accused of hampering attempt to save more than 170 people | Refugees | The Guardian 18 March (accessed 19.3.24)

Habermas, J. (1996) *Between Facts and Norms,* Cambridge: Polity Press

Home Affair Committee (2013) *Asylum,* London: HMSO, HC 71

Home Office (2002) *Secure Borders, Safe Haven,* London: HMSO, CM 5387

Jesuit Refugee Service (2018) *Out in the Cold,* London: Jesuit Refugee Service

Johnson, H.L. [2014] (2018) *Borders, Asylum and Global Non-citizenship,* Cambridge: Cambridge University Press

Joint Committee on Human Rights (2024) *Safety of Rwanda (Asylum and Immigration) Bill*, Second Report of Session 2023–24, 12 February, London: House of Commons and House of Lords, HC 435 HL 62

Kant, I. [1797] (2016) *Perpetual Peace*, Amazon GB

Landolt, P. and L. Goldring (2015) 'Assembling non-citizenship through the work of conditionality' *Citizenship Studies* 19(8):853-69

Lenegan, S. (2023) What safe and legal routes are available for refugees to come to the United Kingdom? – Free Movement 12 July (accessed 4.3.24)

May, T. (2015) 'Speech to the Conservative Party Conference' https://www.independent .co.uk/news/uk/politics/theresa-may-s-speech-to-the-conservative-party -conference-in-full-a6681901.html The Independent 6 October (accessed 28.5.24)

Migration Yorkshire (2022) Nationality and borders ACT 2022 | Migration Yorkshire June (accessed 1.3.24)

Moreno-Lax, V. (2021) 'Protection at sea and the denial of asylum' in *Oxford Handbook of International Refugee Law*, Oxford: Oxford University Press, pp.483–501

Morris, L.D. (1997) 'A cluster of contradictions: the politics of migration in the EU' *Sociology* 31(2): 241-59

Morris, L.D. (2010) *Asylum, Welfare and the Cosmopolitan Ideal*, London: Glasshouse Press

NRPF (2022) Temporary refugee permission introduced | NRPF (nrpfnetwork.org.uk) 11 July (accessed 1.3.24)

NRPF (2023) Illegal migration bill| NRPF (nrpfnetwork.org.uk) 20 July (accessed 28.2.24)

Observer (2023) https://www.theguardian.com/world/2023/apr/29/uk-coastguard-left -channel-migrants-adrift-in-lead-up-to-mass-drowning 29 April (accessed 18.3.24)

Observer (2024) Revealed: UK granted asylum to Rwandan refugees while arguing country was safe | Migration | The Guardian 27 January (accessed 4.3.24)

Observer (2024a) Revealed: UK-funded French forces putting migrants' lives at risk with small-boat tactics | Immigration and asylum | The Guardian 23 March (accessed 24.3.24)

Parliament.UK (2004) *Trends in Asylum Applications*, Select Committee on Home Affairs Second Report, 26 January (accessed 5.3.24)

Pennington, J. (2023) Reflections on the court of appeal's Rwanda decision – Free Movement 5 July (accessed 4.3.24)

Refugee Council (2023) https://www.refugeecouncil.org.uk/wp-content/uploads/2023 /09/The-truth-about-channel-crossings-and-the-impact-of-the-illegal-migration-act -Oct-2023.pdf October (accessed 1.3.24)

Select Committee on Home Affairs (2004) Second Report (parliament.uk) 26 January (accessed 1.3.24)

Social Security Committee (1996) *Benefits for Asylum Seekers*, HC Paper 81

Solf, B. and K. Rehberg (2021) Article: The resettlement gap: A record number of global refugees but few are settled migrationpolicy.org 22 October (accessed 4.3.24)

Squire, V. (2009) *The Exclusionary Politics of Asylum*, London: Palgrave

The Straits Times (2023) Australia allows last refugee on Nauru to leave but retains controversial detention policy | The Straits Times 8 July (accessed 28.2.24)

Straw, J. (2000) *Towards a Common Asylum Procedure*, Speech to the European Conference on Asylum, Lisbon, 16 June

Sturge, G. (2023) *Asylum Statistics*, London: House of Commons Library, SN 01403

UNCLOS (1994) UNCLOS: United Nations Convention on the Law of the Sea 16 November (accessed 13.3.24)

United Nations (1951) Convention relating to the Status of Refugees (189 UNTS 137) | OHCHR (accessed 28.2.24)

Webber, F. (2022) 'Destroying the asylum system' *London Review of Books* 44(7), 7 April

Wilkins, H. (2020) *Refugee Resettlement in the UK,* London: House of Commons Library, BP8750

Yeo, C. (2020) *Welcome to Britain,* London: Biteback Publishing

Yeo, C. (2022) *Refugee Law,* Bristol: Bristol University Press

Yeo, C. (2023) Latest asylum stats show the Home Office failing on all fronts – Free Movement 23 February (accessed 1.3.24)

Yeo (2023a) What is in the Illegal Migration Bill? – Free Movement 8 March (accessed 1.3.24)

Zetter, R. (2007) 'More labels, fewer refugees: Remaking the refugee label in an era of globalisation' *Journal of Refugee Studies* 20(2):172–92

Legal Cases Cited

(Sale v Haitian Centers Council, 509 U.S. 155 (1993)

The Lord Chancellor v Detention Action [2015] EWCA Civ 840

Ghulam and Ors v SSHD [2016] EWHC 2639 (Admin)

ZAT and Ors v SSHD [2016] EWCA Civ 8

NB and Ors v SSHD [2021] EWHC 1489 (Admin)

R(CB) v SSHD [2022] EWHC 3329 (Admin)

AAA and Ors v SSHD [2022] EWHC 3230 (Admin)

AAA and Ors v SSHD [2023] EWCA Civ 745

AAA and Ors v SSHD [2023] UKSC 42

ECPAT UK v Kent County Council and SSHD [2023] EWHC 1953 (Admin)

5 Civic stratification and related debates

The concept of civic stratification, as originally conceived by Lockwood (1996) and as developed in the pages of this volume, amounts to an incipient sociology of rights and as such has the potential to engage and expand a number of related debates. This concluding chapter therefore embarks on a review and elaboration of such linkages, one of which concerns the relationship between citizenship and universal human rights. The former is the subject of Marshall's [1950] (1973) optimistic assessment of the guaranteed inclusion provided by both the formal status and lived experience of full membership in society; the latter, of Arendt's [1948] (1979) pessimistic view that in the absence of citizenship universal human rights were revealed as little more than 'hopeless idealism' or 'feeble-minded hypocrisy' (p.269). Her argument was that until written into domestic law and national constitutions universal rights would lead 'a somewhat shadowy existence as an appeal in individual exceptional cases for which normal legal institutions did not suffice' (p.280–1). Just how human rights have subsequently been framed both in international conventions and in domestic law was also to prove telling, but so too have been the shifting contours of citizenship guarantees. It is with reference to the nuances of both the implementation of universal rights, and the creeping deficiencies of citizenship that the concept of civic stratification can be illuminating, as its concrete effects become apparent[1].

The cosmopolitan promise

While the positive nature of post-national proclamation and cosmopolitan anticipation seemed at first to challenge Arendt's bleak perspective, both have given way to more cautious thinking, and when it comes to their translation on the ground, civic stratification can offer a tool for analysis and understanding of the complexities that emerge. We saw in Chapter 1 how Marshall's model

---

1 Parts of this chapter appeared in my short article 'Multi-layered migration and the cosmopolitan challenge' Queries 2012, 2(8):52–61.delete

DOI: 10.4324/9781003324744-6

of citizenship could fall far short of his vision in delivery, and how this failing offered an entry point for interrogating those rights and provisions associated with the status. Hence, we arrive at the source of Lockwood's (1996:547) argument that: 'while its practice is heavily influenced by the structure of class and status inequality, citizenship can be said to exert a forcefield of its own'. However, in considering the debates to which the concept of civic stratification can make a telling contribution, it is the position and treatment of non-citizens that most readily comes to mind, alongside the limitations of post-national and cosmopolitan argument. Twenty-first century cosmopolitan thinking therefore offers a useful starting point, not least in posing a challenge to the social sciences by calling for a fundamental reconceptualisation of society.

We saw in Chapter 3 that Beck and Sznaider (2006) have questioned the viability of the container image of society associated with a 'methodological nationalism'; that is, an allegedly blinkered position that took the boundaries of society to be synonymous with the boundaries of the nation state, and Marshall's approach could be viewed as an example. It is in this context that Fine (2007) saw cosmopolitanism as entailing both a *de-naturing* and *de-centring* of the nation state, a conceptual reorientation that according to Beck and Sznaider would require a sense of society not as a bounded entity but as a network of social forces and trans-national movements with no clearly delimited geographical home. He therefore argued that the social changes associated with globalisation called for a *cosmopolitan outlook* that can recognise and accommodate the permeability of national borders. However, he distinguished between the normative and the empirical manifestations of such an outlook; the former referring to the level of ideals, and the latter to the extent of actual movement towards a more cosmopolitan society.

The normative content is captured by the notion of the 'world citizen' (Habermas, 2001), which embraces the idea of membership in a world community fuelled by a cosmopolitan empathy and underpinned by the principles of universal human rights (cf. Isin and Turner, 2007). The argument is not that the nation state would be redundant in a new cosmopolitan order, but rather that it would occupy a critical position in building new forms of belonging and entitlement. At the empirical level, however, Beck and Sznaider (2006) recognise that nationalism persists as a co-existing and often conflicting force that may militate against the manifestations of cosmopolitanism. Indeed, Habermas (2001) notes a peculiar tension arising between the universal meaning of human rights and the local conditions of their realisation.

The trans-national migrant is a key figure in this scenario and the tension between cosmopolitan ideals and national interests will often be played out in relation to the position of those who move across national borders. Their presence is significant in a number of ways – they bring fluidity to the constitution of populations on the national territory; they bring cultural difference, which can both challenge and diversify the national identity; and they embody claims to rights which may be rooted outside of national membership. A separate but related aspect of cosmopolitanism is seen in the incorporation of international conventions into domestic law, a development sometimes held to herald both a denationalisation of legitimacy and a reconfiguration of sovereignty (See Meyer et al., 1997; and Levy and Sznaider, 2006). This is one reason why Beck (2006) argued against a dichotomising view that sets external (or cosmopolitan) forces and internal (or national) forces in opposition; he looked rather to an approach that sees the local and the global, or the national and trans-national, as interlocking and mutually constituting phenomena. However, the cosmopolitan project remains conflictual and contested, and involves an obvious uncertainty for trans-national migrants who, despite advances once perceived as signalling an emergent post-national society (Soysal, 1994), do not have access to the full array of citizen rights. So the contemporary position of trans-national migrants and asylum seekers with regard to rights provides a litmus test of how far the situation described by Arendt has now changed, and invites analysis in terms of stratified rights as much as universal rights.

For Benhabib (2004) the very question exposes a dilemma at the heart of liberal democracy, whereby claims to sovereign self-determination co-exist with adherence to the universal principles of human rights. Hence: 'There is not only a tension but often an outright contradiction, between human rights declarations and states' sovereign claims to control their borders as well as to monitor the quality and quantity of admittees' (Benhabib, 2004:2). This has been expressed by Habermas (1998:115) in terms of the 'Janus faced' nature of the nation state: 'Modern democracies act in the name of universal principles that are then circumscribed within a particular civic community'. Given this context, it is often the erosion of state sovereignty that prompts its vigorous reassertion, and hence Grande (2006:104) emphasises the force of migration as a polarising issue in which 'The lowering and unbundling of national boundaries...renders them more salient'. We have seen this demonstrated in the outcome of Britain's 2016 referendum on membership of the European Union, and more recently in attempts to deny asylum seekers access to status determination on British national territory.

While a communitarian approach would seek justification in the fact of already existing social and political communities, and a realist approach would assert the supremacy of political interest over moral constraints, discourse ethics points to the necessity of mediation – between the moral and the political, or in effect between human rights universalism and national particularism. A tension between the two is an inherent aspect of the contemporary nation-state system – rule by a distinctive bounded notion of 'the people', but through processes and institutions that embrace universal principles. Yet in Benhabib's (2004:21) view, modern constitutional democracy is based on the belief that these two commitments can be used to limit each other through what she refers to as democratic iteration. Hence: 'We can render the distinctions between "citizens" and "aliens", "us" and "them", fluid and negotiable through democratic iterations'. However, as Benhabib herself argues, the rights of those present on the territory but lacking full membership of the nation are negotiated on a conflictual terrain where national interests and human rights may come into confrontation. Civic stratification offers a way of understanding and analysing the negotiated compromise that emerges when national closure meets trans-national or 'universal' rights. The ensuing system of stratified statuses with differing access to rights was elaborated in Chapter 3.

Governance and judgment

The exclusion of non-citizens from full political membership reflects what is perhaps the last bastion of citizen privilege, and basic universal rights can indeed be extended beyond national belonging. However, they operate with a legitimate hierarchy of absolute, limited and qualified rights; absolute rights will always involve difficult questions of interpretation, while limited or qualified rights offer scope for equivocation in the name of national interests. Here we come to the pivotal aspect of civic stratification, the role of rights as a form of governance, for differentiated access to rights has been a central plank of attempts by national governments to control trans-national migration. Throughout the post-war period, the member states of Europe have been faced with a set of conflictual issues, and thus control over welfare and the labour market sit alongside labour demand and a commitment to human rights, which can be restricted but rarely completely denied (Morris, 2003). One of the ways in which individual member states, as well as the European Union as a whole, have attempted to manage these multiple influences has been by the designation of varied legal statuses with different rights attached, in other words, by a system of civic stratification.

In Chapter 1 we noted Lockwood's (1996:536) statement that: 'In contemporary capitalist democracies, the ethos and practice of citizenship is at least as likely as class relations to structure group interests and thereby fields of conflict and discontent', and the argument applies even more strongly to the conferral of rights on non-citizens. We have seen this in the varying conditions of access to national territory, and to rights of residence, work and welfare, whose purpose is both to encourage desirable categories of migrants, while discouraging others. However, where the rights at issue engage universal principles, and especially where those principles have been enshrined in domestic law, then the universal and the particular come together in an often indeterminate manner. It is in this context that Jacobson (1997:106) has noted a massive increase in judicial activism, to argue that: 'The state is now a forum where trans-national laws and norms are administered, mediated, and enforced'.

In some respects this view represents a variant of the post-national argument, seeing state legitimacy to be rooted less in popular sovereignty than in international human rights, such that sovereignty in practice becomes secondary to the jurisdiction of the courts. Jacobson, however, argues that this development is not necessarily driven by intrinsic normative concerns, but operates in a piecemeal way, and through a series of ad hoc accommodations that nevertheless reflect a shifting locus of legitimacy. He therefore concludes that these accommodations do not constitute an emergent global society, and instead we find an echo of the civic stratification argument in his recognition that 'social distinctions are becoming ever more multifarious' (Jacobson, 1997:134). The judiciary thus comes to occupy a central position in mediating the tension between post-national universalism and national particularism, while the courts as a deliberative forum can offer a participatory space for those excluded from the national polity (see Habermas, 1996). Such legal procedure, especially where universal commitments have been written into domestic law, provides support for Beck's (2006) endeavour to break with a dichotomising view that sets the global and the national in opposition, and to see the national and trans-national as interlocking and mutually constituting phenomena.

However, a focus on the judicial process as a form of procedural deliberation (Habermas, 1996) draws our attention to the extent of indeterminacy with respect to the content and boundary of rights, which is especially to the fore in developing areas of law, such as universal human rights (Dworkin, 2005). Judgment does not stand apart from social and political life but may both be shaped by and seek to shape prevailing social norms and values, and there is considerable scope for deliberative disagreement to take place both within the judiciary and between the judicial and executive branches of government. Examples of this three-cornered dialogue can be found in varied instances of extended judicial deliberation over aspects of government policy directed towards immigration control – recent cases have involved a challenge to the raised minimum income requirement for family unification, especially with respect to the rights of the child, or the point at which the NRPF rule risks driving a lawfully present foreign parent into destitution, the appropriate minimum standards of maintenance for asylum seekers, and Britain's attempts to remove asylum seekers who enter national territory by irregular means to face status determination and resettlement in Rwanda. Such cases variously involve questions about permissible conditions attached to different categories of legal status, and the extent to which notionally universal rights can be constrained with respect to national interest. Hence, all engage the practice of civic stratification.

This configuration of rights as a form of governance that will often engage questions of judgment also applies to the rights associated with citizenship. We saw in Chapter 2 that conditionality is a prominent and growing feature of welfare systems seeking to influence the behaviour of claimants, especially with respect to availability and readiness for paid employment. We have also seen how claimants have increasingly turned to universal guarantees as a means of challenging the erosions or conditions that apply to some of their citizens' rights. Here we see again how the role of rights as a form of governance can be understood through the conditions attached to different categories of claimant, and the role of legal challenge and judicial deliberation in determining the content of rights and the limits of conditionality. All raise issues that can be helpfully illustrated and elaborated with reference to the concept of civic stratification.

Rights and recognition

Alongside the deployment of rights and their associated conditional requirements as a mode of governance, there is another conceptual terrain that can be advanced by the notion of civic stratification, and that is rights as recognition. It has long been argued that the significance of rights reaches beyond legal guarantees to stand as a marker of social status and belonging, and hence of recognition. An early example of this position is to be found in the work of T.H.Marshall [1950] (1973) and his seminal essay on *"Citizenship and Social Rights"*, which is about the role of rights in confirming equal social standing, or what would now be termed recognition. Though his focus is on citizenship as the marker of membership in society, Marshall's writing has a broader application in helping to think about the role of rights as an expression of social worth: 'a kind of basic human equality associated with the concept of full membership of the community' (p.6). Indeed, he makes the interesting claim that a degree of class inequality can be tolerated provided that it does not cut too deep, and that equality of status is assured.

We have seen how Marshall has been criticised for his failure to consider the exclusionary aspects of citizenship that come into play in relation to trans-national migration, and there is now a set of more pressing questions in relation to rights and recognition, for: 'In the cosmopolitan constellation sociology is...concerned with the formation of post-national and cross-national bonds, or who belongs and who does not, and how inclusion and exclusion arise' (Beck and Sznaider, 2006:400). Charles Taylor (1994) offers the best known linkage between rights and recognition in relation to the position of minority groups, and his work was important in two ways; firstly, in seeing collective cultures as closely tied to the personal identity of group members, and secondly, in seeing the affirmation of a right to difference (through cultural rights) as a form of social recognition. The absence of such recognition is argued to inflict damage on the individual's sense of self and self-worth, and therefore on their identity, in a form of *mis*-recognition. Taylor ties this linkage to a broader development in the terrain of rights, also apparent in Marshall's work, and manifest in the move from ascription to universalism, a sentiment echoed in post-national argument. Hence: 'with the movement from honour to dignity has come a politics of universalism, emphasising the equal dignity of all citizens' (Taylor, 1994:37). In an important alternative to assimilationist approaches to minority groups, Taylor argues that toleration of difference is insufficient for recognition without some more positive valuing of diversity as of worth in its own right.

Despite the hugely significant impact of Taylor's argument, it has two limitations for thinking about the position of migrants: firstly, it is confined to cultural rights, and raises the question of whether the argument about recognition and mis-recognition can apply to other aspects of entitlement; secondly, writing with the position of French Canadians in mind, he makes repeated reference to equality and dignity for all *citizens.* So an interesting question arises as to the dynamic of recognition beyond cultural rights, and with reference to trans-national migrants who do not possess the full status of citizenship. Here we can look to work by Axel Honneth (1995:14) that is concerned with a much broader array of rights and, like Marshall's essay, postulates that full membership in a rights-granting community amounts to a form of moral approbation and is hence a marker of social worth. Honneth (1995:12–3) therefore starts from a view of rights as grounded in citizenship, and rooted in his conception of society as 'an ethically integrated community of free citizens' that shapes the individual's sense of self-worth through a recognition of their positive contribution to society.

In this argument, the granting of rights through membership is based on a set of requirements that reflect the conditions for belonging and thus carry an idealised notion of the good citizen, while conversely a denial of membership and rights will carry the opposite connotation. There are therefore two dimensions of rights at work; rights as flowing from a formal legal status of citizenship, and rights as expressive of the informal conferral of social esteem. It is in the context of this second dimension of rights that Honneth (1995:122) speaks of the 'social medium' within which the law operates and also of 'supplemental cultural interpretations' (p.126) of social worth. Although Honneth has been criticised for the 'unacceptable communitarian baggage' (Fraser, 2003:10) that this theory carries, an analysis of rights in communitarian terms does not necessarily imply its endorsement. Indeed, Honneth sees the establishment of universal human rights as the final stage of a longer process of development documented in Marshall's chronological account of citizenship rights – away from ascription and towards inclusion.

While for Marshall the inclusionary dimension of rights was addressed through the internal functioning of citizenship, Honneth sees the logical conclusion of a move away from ascription to be the institutionalisation of universal human rights. He is also interested in the possibility that the social experience of disrespect could generate struggles for recognition through rights, and one example may be found when groups excluded from full citizenship and its associated rights make a claim to rights based on universal guarantees. In practice, such claims are usually made on their behalf by civic activists (NGOs and legal advocates) who take up the cause of those located on the margins of civic inclusion/exclusion. Recent British examples are the asylum seekers threatened with removal to Rwanda, or migrants lawfully present as principal carers of citizen children but forced into destitution by the no recourse to public funds condition, or victims of the Windrush scandal, etc.

These and other examples are instances of the deployment of rights as a tool of governance, since wherever there are conditions attached to the granting of a right, there will also be opportunities for monitoring and surveillance in its administration. In this process, the treatment that groups or individuals receive at the hands of officialdom will often reflect or be reflected by shifting public perceptions of social worth, and again, the idea of civic stratification is helpful. As we have seen, Lockwood distinguishes between two axes of civic stratification: the formal dimension expressed in terms of the presence or absence of a right; and the informal dimension expressed in terms of gain or deficit (as rooted in privilege or stigma) that affect the actual enjoyment of a right. These two dimensions of civic stratification are similar to Honneth's distinction between legal status and social esteem, and both writers concur in seeing a dominant value scheme to be operative in the functioning of rights.

Moral resources

Of central importance are what Lockwood (1996:536) terms the 'moral and material resources' that claimants can bring to bear in accessing their rights; such resources can enhance existing entitlement, and may also underpin mobilisations for the expansion of rights by a given group. However, we have seen how the reverse dynamic is also possible, such that the discrediting of a group may serve as a prelude to reducing their rights,[2] as in the construction of the bogus asylum seeker. In other words, there is an interesting interaction between the formal and informal aspects of civic stratification, which may be implicated in both expansive and restrictive changes in any given regime of rights. Honneth's interest in the experience of disrespect as a motivating force behind the claim to rights by those outside of citizenship is obviously relevant here. For them, a question remains as to how far membership of the community of humanity can secure basic human rights, or better put, how far have we moved from the time of Arendt's [1948] (1979) dismal judgement on the scope for supra-national universals. In fact, the constitution of liberal democracy is not quite the paradox it is presented as being – if the commitment to universals is confined to members of the national community via national

2 For a fuller working through of this argument see Morris (2010).

citizenship, then they are not universals at all, but become a terrain of struggle for outsiders on national territory.

While Honneth looks to the experience of disrespect as a motivating factor in claims to greater recognition through rights, Lockwood notes that the stigma attaching to certain groups may well have a disabling effect on their potential to mobilise for change. However, a number of writers (e.g. Lockwood, 1996; Schneider and Ingram, 1993; Alexander, 2006) have predicted increasing recourse to legal action, and Lockwood remarks on the role of civic activists in taking up the cause of society's most vulnerable groups. Habermas (1996:371) has also noted a possible role for the courts in providing one forum for translating the concept of deliberative democracy into more sociological terms. He sees the organisations and movements of civil society to be active both in shaping public opinion and in serving as advocates for neglected issues and under-represented groups, thus providing a *lifeworld* anchor for the public sphere.

In Habermas's (1996:383) model for the functioning of the public sphere, conflicts can be brought from the periphery of political concern to the centre, provided there is a sufficiently vital civil society in operation that can appeal not only to office holders and the legislature, but to the critical judgment of a public of citizens. However, where public support cannot be invoked, where vulnerable groups are excluded from direct representation in the polity, and where fundamental rights are at issue, then legal action may provide a way forward. These interests come close to Alexander's (2006) focus on the sources of social solidarity, but his work gives greater emphasis to the contradictory and fragmented nature of 'real' civil societies, which he argues can be as repressive as they are liberating. In this context, Alexander also notes the dual functioning of the legal system both as a tool for the coercive power of class, caste or state and as a means by which such power may be challenged, through a process of 'civil repair'.

A potentially related literature has grown up around the notion of 'moral economy', which offers a complementary approach to Lockwood's notion of moral resources, as one pressing question concerns the foundation, elaboration and dissemination of the underpinning value frame. We have seen how Thompson's (1971) original argument considered the emergence of a moral economy 'from below', as related to demands that 18th century landowners live up to their moral obligations in securing survival for all. We have also noted that this perspective has been reversed in contemporary theorising, based on the argument that all economies are moral economies (Booth, 1994; Sayer, 2007; Clarke and Newman, 2012) in that all rely on some underlying moral frame. In this light, we have seen how a moral economy can be imposed from above in terms of the dominant discourse at play in the fashioning of a regime of rights, illustrating Munch's (2012) argument on the role of political rhetoric. It not only shapes the popular perception of a problem but also determines what is deemed an appropriate policy response, making manifest one answer to Douglas's (1986) question of 'how institutions think'.

The moral economy of rights

A broadening out of the focus of moral economy is central to much of the work of Didier Fassin (2009:15) who understands the concept as the mental state of a collectivity that is 'historically created, modified and destroyed'. The general context for this reconfigured notion of moral economy is his own research programme for a 'critical moral anthropology', which starts from the observation that despite an early interest in the moral dimension of social life as part of the founding project of the social sciences, morality has by convention fallen to the terrain of philosophers. Fassin, however, considers that the time is ripe for a change in orientation, reflecting a broader trend in contemporary society whereby moral evaluations and justifications have become more central to the public sphere. However, the revival of interest in moral issues lies less with 'pure' moral dilemmas and more with a blurring of boundaries, whereby moral rationale seeps into political, legal and economic spheres of governance. This is especially the case in relation to how the most marginalised, stigmatised and discriminated groups are treated by the formal institutions of society. He cites migrants and minorities as the most obvious targets for 'morally' driven intervention, though Fassin's own work also extends to welfare provisions, asking how moral categories are used to 'disqualify or absolve' when defining the boundaries of inclusion and exclusion. The scientific challenge he looks to lies in the mutual interchange between political discourse, public policy and professional practices, and one focus for such a project would be the construction of categories of desert, and how they find their way into public sentiment and public policy. There is an echo here of Douglas' (1986) question as to 'how institutions think', while the analytical task for Fassin (2012:12) is to 'seize morals at the point where they are articulated with politics'.

In Lockwood's model, expansionary movement within a regime of rights is primarily driven by moral resources, but these themselves are socially constructed, and we have seen in the substantive chapters of the present book that rights can also contract. Fassin (2005:365) approaches this issue in terms of a 'paradigmatic tension' between the discourses and practices of compassion and repression, or the politics of pity and the politics of control. The outcome in terms of rights and protections is then viewed through the 'values and hierarchies of values' (p.366) mobilised by the state to fashion a socially acceptable form of repression in the management of 'undesired and suffering others'. This is achieved, according to Fassin, through 'the performative power of words' (p.375), which in the example of asylum seekers has justified the reduction of social rights, the criminalisation of their presence, and the increasing precarity of the protection offered. A similar analysis could apply to the contraction of welfare rights for needy citizens – both the unemployed and also the long-term sick and disabled.

In fact, a subsequent article by Fassin (2009:para 37) offers the following definition of moral economy as: 'The production, distribution and use of moral sentiments, emotions and values, norms and obligations in social space', but we could add to this 'and their systematic incorporation into economic relations'. This composite definition then foregrounds the actual production of moral sentiment, its circulation, and its embedding within policy and practice, and as Fassin notes, this can be a shifting configuration that mobilises emotions and values as well as norms and obligations. Thus Fassin argues that 'moral economies are unstable…fluid realities traversed by tensions and contradictions' (para 47) that are open to change and negotiation, and it is this process that is recognised by Lockwood's (1996) notion of civic expansion. So the analytical and critical strengths of this reworked concept of moral economy are advanced in the notion of civic stratification, a concept that not only provides a vocabulary for describing the outcome but also advances our understanding of the underlying dynamic process. Fassin writes of a hierarchical conception of lives which is also a hierarchical conception of human beings; Lockwood's framework shows how this hierarchy also translates into a stratified system for the granting and/or delivery of rights.

Once political intent is built into this picture, we can seen how such a dynamic comes to shape the public view of distinctive social groupings and to determine the accrual or otherwise of moral resources that could enhance their claim to rights (as in civic expansion). This process is at work not only in conceptions of the worthy migrant, or 'genuine' asylum seeker, but also of the 'good citizen', increasingly cast in terms of ability to serve the needs of the labour market, with corresponding exclusionary measures for groups who cannot meet this requirement (for a UK example see Morris, 2007, 2021). In both cases the interaction of formal entitlement and informal moral standing is a key issue that turns on the question of desert and while differential desert is itself a much documented phenomenon, the concept of civic stratification and its internal operation can throw light on this argument and a set of related debates.

In advancing a view that is similar to aspects of Fassin's work, Bridget Anderson (2013:2) argues that borders are not simply territorial but reach into the heart of political space such that laws on citizenship and migration produce rather than reflect differing status positions. She construes debates about migration as essentially debates about the 'community of value' – which might mean both what is deemed to be of value to society, and also what set of values a society itself adheres to. In this configuration, Anderson argues that the community of value is defined from the outside by the non-citizen and from the inside by the failed citizen, and Fassin's notion of an ongoing tension between compassion and repression will be detectable in each of these boundaries. Such boundary drawing is structured by the classifications devised by policymakers, which in turn are subject to constraints dictated by the 'community of value', and often apparent in the detail of conditionality that determines access to the rights at issue. Furthermore, these distinctions are reflections of 'how institutions think' (Douglas, 1986) and are also the basis for what have been termed 'bordering' practices in social and geographical space.

Bordering

The concept of bordering turns a noun into a verb and is driven by the recognition that the policing of nation state borders is no longer confined (if it was ever) to a physical location but has an extra-territorial reach that is manifest in airports, rail terminals, consulates and other external checkpoints. National borders have thus been deterritorialised (Yuval-Davis et al., 2019), but at the same time they have also been internalised, as checks and controls are written ever more firmly into the daily practice of national and local state institutions (see, for example Morris, 1998). One of the more extreme manifestations of this latter process was the explicit 'hostile environment' approach adopted in Britain in 2016, which ultimately gave rise to the Windrush scandal (as detailed in Chapter 3). In a more general sense, the notion of bordering is closely associated with the reassertion of national sovereignty in the face of powerful global institutions, security fears, and the multiple forces that compel people to seek opportunities or protection away from their country of birth.

The most significant aspect of this conceptualisation of bordering lies in treating physical locations and national identities as actively constructed and maintained rather than given, such that: 'borders need to be seen as constitutive parts of the world rather than as segmenting a pre-given 'natural' whole' (Yuval-Davis et al., 2019:4). Hence borders are something more than physical dividing lines, but are written into symbolic, social and cultural lines of inclusion and exclusion that pervade everyday interactions and are governed by an increasing array of technologies and ideologies. Hence: 'bordering has a double character, as a political project of governance and a political project of belonging' (Yuval-Davis et al., 2019:5), and since access to and control of resources are of central concern we soon arrive at the terms of entry, presence and stay on a national territory, or the matter of rights and duties. The differential allocation of rights and duties is in turn underpinned by a process Van Houtum and Van Naerssen (2002) refer to as 'bordering, ordering and othering', and it then takes only a small step to view the outcome in terms of a system of civic stratification. So we might ask in what ways do the concepts of bordering and of civic stratification differ, and can they be viewed as complementary.

Certainly both terms broadly speaking refer to the same phenomena. Although Lockwood's (1996) original concept of civic stratification was largely looking inwards to the inequalities generated by the rights and duties associated with citizenship, we have seen how the idea applies just as well, or even better, to the varied experience of non-citizens. So both 'bordering' and 'civic stratification' have been taken up as ways of understanding and analysing the increasingly complex phenomenon of cross-border movement and its management by sovereign nation states. Bordering is the broader of the two concepts and looks both to the changing global forces that drive trans-national migration, and to individual experience as mediated by political discourse and devices of control. In fact, it might be said that the concept of bordering focuses on the ways that borders follow people, expanding the moment of control from the external borders between nations to the daily interactions that occur between citizens and non-citizens, and in every occasion of exposure to authority and legality. This is so much the case that scope for social solidarity and cohesion is argued to be disrupted by the suspicion and fear that circulates both within and between families and communities (Yuval-Davis et al., 2019).

But, as noted, bordering is also focused on a range of individual experiences that flow from the differential treatment of varied categories of migrant, and on tracing the nature and effects of relationships that are maintained with the country of origin. The focus of interest is therefore on the whole social and economic configuration that surrounds, facilitates and manages cross-border experiences, on migrants variable access to resources, and also on the political objectives and discourse that shape the phenomenon. So bordering is concerned with how the imagined territorial border extends outwards to distant visa offices and airport check-ins, but also extends inwards to affect almost all social encounters. Of particular interest are the 'grey spaces', which take a variety of forms – vast official waiting rooms where refugees queue for resettlement, informal camps that spring up around critical crossing points, detention centres where they await expulsion, or extra-territorial (offshore) processing camps.

Grey zones are also operative when irregular migrants fear claiming those minimal rights that they might possess (such as employer obligations to workers) because such a claim would expose them to control checks and likely deportation, or when their exclusion from formally renting property exposes them to highly constrained living conditions, etc. But more than this, their whole life is lived in the shadows, under a constant fear of detection or exposure, and most especially so if they are visibly 'different' and therefore more likely to be a target of suspicion (Block et al., 2014). It is also commonly the case that this pall of suspicion affects many migrants who are lawfully present and thus has repercussions beyond the original design of specific policies, as was amply illustrated in the case of the UK's 'hostile environment'. These negative effects were often felt not only by the people who were targetted (and sometimes mistakenly so) but also by those who were required to implement the checks, most notably landlords and employers, and the discriminatory impact of such policy was successfully demonstrated in Britain's High Court, although the Court of Appeal accepted the government's argument that this was justifiable in terms of their overall objectives (JCWI v SSHD [2020] EWCA Civ 542).

We can see from the comments above that 'bordering' and 'civic stratification' are concepts that occupy similar terrain and address similar questions – so are they the same thing? It seems that the former concept casts its net wider than civic stratification, to take in shifting influences from the global to the local, and in doing so is particularly attuned to the lived experience, and most especially the negative consequences of bordering practices. Civic stratification is more narrowly focused as a concept, and was described at the beginning of this chapter as a potential framework for the sociology of rights. However, this analytical frame does incorporate not only the legal dimension of formal entitlement but the influence of moral and material resources in shaping access, and also in driving the dynamic of expansion or contraction of rights for particular groups, or across a whole regime of rights.

When civic stratification is also linked to the way that a discourse of morality can be embedded in political parlance, we see how it filters through to the detail of policy design and fosters corresponding public sentiment. It also offers a key to understanding how the circuits of gain or deficit, and expansion or contraction function. Furthermore, the focus on access to rights and the possibility of civic activism also directs attention to the scope for legal challenge as the courts become a forum for deliberation and interpretation of rights that can sometimes override government intent. It therefore illustrates and amplifies our understanding of the 'bordering' process, and can drill down into the detail of how political discourse, policy design and legal entitlement are interlinked or on occasion called into question. So while 'bordering' addresses the macro and micro level, civic stratification occupies the meso level that mediates between the two, even to the point of addressing possible mobility upwards or downwards through the hierarchy of statuses.

Bare life and degrees of exclusion

Giorgio Agamben's [1995] (1998) use of the concept of 'bare life' is highly evocative and has sparked some imaginative interpretations and responses (eg. Sigona, 2015; Huysmans, 2008) in applying the concept to exclusion from the 'polis', and hence to the bottom rung on the ladder of civic stratification. In this sense the spectre of bare life reflects Arendt's [1948] (1979:299) characterisation of the absence of citizenship as 'the abstract nakedness of being nothing but human'. For Agamben (1998:7) the condition of bare life becomes the constitutive outside of society such that 'western politics first constitutes itself through an exclusion (which is simultaneously an inclusion)', and so bare life is counterposed in this configuration to 'politically qualified life'. The argument then leads him to the assertion that the simultaneous exclusion and capturing of bare life amounts to the hidden foundation of the entire political system (1998:9). Hence, the idea of a space 'outside' of society – the camp – as created through a suspension of the juridical order and therefore as a space of exception, seems to map onto the circumstances of the asylum seekers confined to official or unofficial waiting rooms that often precede access to a national territory and the possibility of actually realising protection.

Despite the intuitive appeal of Agamben's elaboration of the notion of bare life, there has been a growing caution about applying it too literally to an extant situation. Agamben (1998:131) himself seems to have anticipated this in his reference to 'the constant need to redefine the threshold in life that distinguishes and separates what is inside from what is outside', as bare life becomes politicised by the declaration of rights. He also notes that the various metamorphoses of 'the camp' mean 'it is now securely lodged within the city's interior' (p.176) – but we are left to imagine what sociopolitical processes might lie behind these developments.

Huymans' (2008:166) strong reservations about the 'idiom of exception' as applied to the notion and actuality of the camp are that: 'exceptionalist readings of political power tend to politically neutralise the societal as a realm of multi-faceted, historically structured political mediations and mobilizations'. So among his objections to Agamben's approach is that the category of 'life' (whether bare life or qualified life) displaces societal categories that actually render life social, and in doing so seeks to 'ontologically erase' (p.175) sociopolitical struggles and to act on the body simply as physical life. This is achieved to the neglect of societal mediations, and in the context of non-citizens such struggles commonly revolve around access to territory, access to resources, and access to rights, in which civic activists feature most prominently *via* legal interventions and public campaigning.

Sigona (2015) has also questioned Agamben's representation of 'the camp' and points to multi-faceted mediations and mobilisations that penetrate even life in the 'camp', noting the presence of hierarchies or degrees of inclusion. The environment of the camp itself while undoubtedly generating its own brutalities can also create a world rich in social relations of mutual recognition and support, as well as networks that extend beyond its boundaries. Other writers (Chauvin and Garces-Mascarenas, 2012) have shown how undocumented status is not necessarily an absolute marker but can be rendered a temporary condition by accumulated emblems of desert, while Landolt and Goldring (2015) also note that boundaries within and between categories of citizen and non-citizen are never fixed or impermeable. In fact they recognise that the classificatory regime incorporates a system of 'chutes and ladders', whereby individuals can experience upward or downward mobility in relation to the terms of their presence and their access to rights. Mezzadra and Neilson (2012:60) introduce a further refinement through the notion of topology, which they apply to the 'different kinds of folding and filtering that challenge the rigidity of the distinctions between inclusion and exclusion'.

All of these reflections and reservations about bare life and the nature and extent of exclusions have a potential link to the concept of civic stratification, as a major mediating factor that connects bare life to qualified life is the system of differential statuses that determines access to rights. This system also contains the rules of transition for moving up (or down) the hierarchy, and the dynamics of civic expansion or contraction help to address the mediating factors involved. We have seen that expansion is commonly advanced through the intervention of civic activists, and in turn enhanced by the mobilisation of moral resources. Equally, a political attack on the moral standing of a given group can be implicated in the erosion of moral standing and contraction of rights, and so again the civic stratification framework functions at the meso level to elaborate a range of partial inclusions or exclusions.

But as a number of commentators observe (eg. Landolt and Goldring, 2015; Chauvin and Garces-Macarenas, 2012), these dynamics can also apply to citizenship itself, which is of course made clear in Lockwood's original conception of civic stratification. In fact, Turner (2024:171) argues that we have been witness to an erosion of citizenship whereby 'we are all denizens now', and one key aspect of this argument relates to the shrinking guarantees of social citizenship. In Marshall's model social rights are the key to 'the right to live the life of a civilised being according to the standards prevailing in the society' (p.72), though as we saw in Chapter 2, conditionality can escalate to such an extent that the outcome is destitution and even death (Morris, 2020). So the 'failed citizen' in Anderson's (2013) terms, joins those other groups who are pushed to the outer limits of protection, as bare life comes to infiltrate the basic fabric of society.

The erosion of citizenship

The full implications of Turner's argument, however, are that the Marshallian model of citizenship has been undermined in a more general sense by 'market fundamentalism' (Somers, 2008), as neo-liberal economic policies erode the tax base of the state. He also adds that conscription as a duty of citizenship is now quite rare among more developed countries. So as the balance between income tax and indirect tax shifts away from the former and towards the latter, and the notion of a citizen army is no longer applicable, then the shared experience of being a citizen tends to wither away. Hence, Turner (2024:78) argues that citizens experience their relation with the state and the market as passive consumers of decisions made by a political class over which they have little control and with which they have little connection – so that the active citizen is replaced by the consumer denizen.

Turner does note that a citizen may break the law without risking deportation, while this is less true for denizens, but even this distinction is blurring. We have seen how in British law it is now possible to strip someone of their citizenship without prior notification if this is deemed to be in the public interest, and if an alternative citizenship could be available. Of course, there is a stratified element to this measure, which will for the most part affect second or third-generation migrants. Furthermore, full citizenship is argued by Turner to be increasingly reserved for the employed and the employable, while for many citizens, the experience of work in a flexible and uncertain labour market is closer to that of a denizen, especially if social rights are shrinking. The more mobile labour becomes in this picture, then the greater the problems associated with a residential foundation for social and legal membership. So we begin to see a closing of the gap between migrants and citizens, but not in the manner anticipated by post-national or cosmopolitan predictions; it is not so much that migrants come to resemble citizens but that citizens come to resemble denizens. Indeed, the less privileged members of society are increasingly likely to fall back on claims to universal human rights where their citizens' rights fail them (Morris, 2016), while access to rights will itself be increasingly shaped by the possession of moral or material resources.

References

Agamben, G. [1995] (1998) *Homo Sacer*, Stanford: Stanford University Press

Alexander, J.C. (2006) *The Civil Sphere*, Oxford: Oxford University Press

Anderson, B. (2013) *Us and Them*, Oxford: Oxford University Press

Arendt, H. [1948] (1979) *The Origins of Totalitarianism*, New York: Harcourt Brace

Beck, U. (2006) *Cosmopolitan Vision*, Cambridge: Polity Press

Beck, U. and N. Sznaider (2006) 'Unpacking cosmopolitanism for the social sciences' *British Journal of Sociology* 57(1):1–23

Benhabib, S. (2004) *The Rights of Others*, Cambridge: Cambridge University Press

Block, A., N. Sigona and R. Zetter (2014) *Sans Papier: The Social and Economic Lives of Young Undocumented Migrants*, London: Pluto Press

Booth, W.J. (1994) 'On the idea of the moral economy' *American Political Science Review* 88(3):653–67

Chauvin, S. and B. Garces-Mascarenas (2012) 'Beyond informal citizenship' *International Political Sociology* 6(3):241–59

Clarke, J. and S. Newman (2012) 'The alchemy of austerity' *Critical Social Policy* 32(3):299–319

Douglas, M. (1986) *How Institutions Think*, Syracuse: Syracuse University Press

Dworkin, R. [1977] (2005) *Taking Rights Seriously*, London: Duckworth

Fassin, D. (2005) 'Compassion and repression' *American Anthropological Association* 20(3):362–87

Fassin, D. (2009) 'Moral economy revisited' *Annales. Histoire. Sciences Sociales* 64(6):1237–66

Fassin, D. (2012) *Humanitarian Reason*, Berkley and Los Angeles: University of California Press

Fine, R. (2007) *Cosmopolitanism*, Abingdon: Routledge

Fraser, N. (2003) 'Social justice in the age of identity politics' in N. Fraser and A. Honneth (eds.) *Redistribution or Recognition*, London: Verso

Grande, E. (2006) 'Cosmopolitan political science' *British Journal of Sociology* 57(1):87–111

Habermas, J. (1996) *Between Facts and Norms*, Cambridge: Polity Press

Habermas, J. (1998) *Inclusion of the Other*, Cambridge: Polity Press

Habermas, J. (2001) *The Post-national Constellation*, Cambridge: Polity Press

Honneth, A. (1995) *The Struggle for Recognition*, Cambridge: Polity Press

Huysmans, J. (2008) 'The jargon of exception' *International Political Sociology* 2(2):165–83

Isin, E.F. and B.S. Turner (2007) 'Investigating citizenship' *Citizenship Studies* 11(1):5–17

Jacobson, D. (1997) *Rights Across Borders: Immigration and the Decline of Citizenship*, Baltimore, MD: Johns Hopkins University Press

Landolt, P. and L. Goldring (2015) 'Assembling non-citizenship through the work of conditionality' *Citizenship Studies* 19(8):853–69

Levy, D. and N. Sznaider (2006) 'Sovereignty transformed: a sociology of human rights' *British Journal of Sociology* 57(4): 657-76

Lockwood, D. (1996) 'Civic integration and class formation' *British Journal of Sociology* 47(3):531–50

Marshall, T.H. [1950] (1973) 'Citizenship and social class' in *Class, Citizenship and Social Development*, New York: Doubleday and Co., pp.65–122

Meyer, J., J. Boli, G.M. Thomas and F.O. Ramirez (1997) 'World society and the nation state' *American Journal of Sociology* 103(1):144–81

Mezzadra, S. and B. Neilson (2012) 'Between inclusion and exclusion' *Theory, Culture and Society* 29(4/5):58–75

Morris, L.D. (1998) 'Governing at a distance' *International Migration Review* 32(4):949–73

Morris, L.D. (2003) 'Managing contradiction' *International Migration Review* 37(1):74–100

Morris, L.D. (2007) 'New labour's community of rights' *Journal of Social Policy* 36(1):39–57

Morris, L.D. (2010) 'Civic stratification and the cosmopolitan ideal' *European Societies* 11(4):603–24

Morris, L.D. (2012a) 'Multi-layered migration and the cosmopolitan challenge' *Queries* 2(8):52–61

Morris, L.D. (2016) 'Squaring the circle: Domestic welfare, migration and human rights' *Citizenship Studies* 20(6–7):693–709

Morris, L.D. (2020) 'The topology of welfare-migration-asylum: Britain's outsiders inside' *Journal of Poverty and Social Justice* 28(2):245–64

Morris, L.D. (2021) *The Moral Economy of Welfare and Migration: Reconfiguring Rights in Austerity Britain*, London: McGill-Queens University Press

Munch, R. (2012) *Inclusion and Exclusion in the Liberal Competition State*, Abingdon: Routledge

Sayer, A. (2007) 'Moral economy as critique' *New Political Economy* 12(2):261–70

Schnieder, A. and H. Ingram (1993) 'The social construction of target populations' *American Political Science Review* 87(2):334–47

Sigona, N. (2015) 'Campzenship' *Citizenship Studies* 19(1):1–15

Somers, M. (2008) *Genealogies of Citizenship,* Cambridge: Cambridge University Press

Soysal, Y. (1994) *Limits of Citizenship,* Chicago: University of Chicago Press

Taylor, C. (1994) 'The politics of recognition' in A. Gutman (ed.) *Multiculturalism,* Princeton NJ: Princeton University Press, pp.25–73

Thompson, E.P. (1971) 'The moral economy of the English crowd in the eighteenth century' *Past and Present* 50(Feb):76–136

Turner, B.S. (2024) 'We are all denizens now' in *The Rise and Fall of Citizenship,* Abingdon: Routledge, pp.171–86

Van Houtum, H. and T. Van Naerssen (2002) 'Bordering, ordering and othering' *Journal of Economic and Social Geography* 93(2):125–36

Yuval-Davis, N., G. Wemyss and K. Cassidy (2019) *Bordering,* Cambridge: Polity Press

Legal Cases Cited

JCWI v SSHD [2020] EWCA Civ 542

Index

For Product Safety Concerns and Information please contact our EU
representative GPSR@taylorandfrancis.com
Taylor & Francis Verlag GmbH, Kaufingerstraße 24, 80331 München, Germany